Sexual Orientation and Society

ISSUES

Volume 153

Series Editor

Lisa Firth

Independence

First published by Independence
The Studio, High Green
Great Shelford
Cambridge CB22 5EG
England

© Independence 2008

Photocopy licence
The material in this book is protected by copyright. However, the
purchaser is free to make multiple copies of particular articles for instructional
purposes for immediate use within the purchasing institution.
Making copies of the entire book is not permitted.

British Library Cataloguing in Publication Data
Sexual Orientation and Society – (Issues Series)
I. Firth, Lisa II. Series
306.7'6

ISBN 978 1 86168 440 0

Printed in Great Britain
MWL Print Group Ltd

Cover
The illustration on the front cover is by
Simon Kneebone.

CONTENTS

Chapter One: Sexuality Issues

Chapter Two: Sexuality and the Law

Useful information for readers

Dear Reader,

Issues: Sexual Orientation and Society

Homosexuality was decriminalised in England and Wales in 1967, yet issues such as gay adoption and civil partnerships are still considered contentious. Many gay people will also suffer misunderstanding, discrimination and homophobic abuse during their lives. This title contains articles on topics including homophobic bullying, teaching about sexuality in schools, the portrayal of gay people in the media and the adoption debate.

The purpose of Issues

Sexual Orientation and Society is the one hundred and fifty-third volume in the **Issues** series. The aim of this series is to offer up-to-date information about important issues in our world. Whether you are a regular reader or new to the series, we do hope you find this book a useful overview of the many and complex issues involved in the topic.

Titles in the **Issues** series are resource books designed to be of especial use to those undertaking project work or requiring an overview of facts, opinions and information on a particular subject, particularly as a prelude to undertaking their own research.

The information in this book is not from a single author, publication or organisation; the value of this unique series lies in the fact that it presents information from a wide variety of sources, including:
⇨ Government reports and statistics
⇨ Newspaper articles and features
⇨ Information from think-tanks and policy institutes
⇨ Magazine features and surveys
⇨ Website material
⇨ Literature from lobby groups and charitable organisations.*

Critical evaluation

Because the information reprinted here is from a number of different sources, readers should bear in mind the origin of the text and whether the source is likely to have a particular bias or agenda when presenting information (just as they would if undertaking their own research). It is hoped that, as you read about the many aspects of the issues explored in this book, you will critically evaluate the information presented. It is important that you decide whether you are being presented with facts or opinions. Does the writer give a biased or an unbiased report? If an opinion is being expressed, do you agree with the writer?

Sexual Orientation and Society offers a useful starting point for those who need convenient access to information about the many issues involved. However, it is only a starting point. Following each article is a URL to the relevant organisation's website, which you may wish to visit for further information.

Kind regards,

Lisa Firth
Editor, **Issues** series

** Please note that Independence Publishers has no political affiliations or opinions on the topics covered in the **Issues** series, and any views quoted in this book are not necessarily those of the publisher or its staff.*

Answers to your questions

For a better understanding of sexual orientation and homosexuality

Since 1975, the American Psychological Association has called on psychologists to take the lead in removing the stigma of mental illness that has long been associated with lesbian, gay and bisexual orientations. The discipline of psychology is concerned with the well-being of people and groups and therefore with threats to that well-being. The prejudice and discrimination that people who identify as lesbian, gay or bisexual regularly experience have been shown to have negative psychological effects. This article is designed to provide accurate information for those who want to better understand sexual orientation and the impact of prejudice and discrimination on those who identify as lesbian, gay or bisexual.

> **Sexual orientation refers to an enduring pattern of emotional, romantic and/or sexual attractions to men, women or both sexes**

What is sexual orientation?

Sexual orientation refers to an enduring pattern of emotional, romantic and/or sexual attractions to men, women or both sexes. Sexual orientation also refers to a person's sense of identity based on those attractions, related behaviours, and membership in a community of others who share those attractions. Research over several decades has demonstrated that sexual orientation ranges along a continuum, from exclusive attraction to the other sex to exclusive attraction to the same sex. However, sexual orientation is usually discussed in terms of three categories: heterosexual (having emotional, romantic or sexual attractions to members of the other sex), gay/lesbian (having emotional, romantic or sexual attractions to members of one's own sex), and bisexual (having emotional, romantic or sexual attractions to both men and women). This range of behaviours and attractions has been described in various cultures and nations throughout the world. Many cultures use identity labels to describe people who express these attractions. In the United States the most frequent labels are lesbians (women attracted to women), gay men (men attracted to men) and bisexual people (men or women attracted to both sexes). However, some people may use different labels or none at all.

Sexual orientation is distinct from other components of sex and gender, including biological sex (the anatomical, physiological and genetic characteristics associated with being male or female), gender identity (the psychological sense of being male or female), and social gender role (the cultural norms that define feminine and masculine behaviour).

Sexual orientation is commonly discussed as if it were solely a characteristic of an individual, like biological sex, gender identity or age. This perspective is incomplete because sexual orientation is defined in terms of relationships with others. People express their sexual orientation through behaviours with others, including such simple actions as holding hands or kissing. Thus, sexual orientation is closely tied to the intimate personal relationships that meet deeply felt needs for love, attachment and intimacy. In addition to sexual behaviours, these bonds include nonsexual physical affection between partners, shared goals and values, mutual support and ongoing commitment. Therefore, sexual orientation is not merely a personal characteristic within an individual. Rather, one's sexual orientation defines the group of people in which one is likely to find the satisfying and fulfilling romantic relationships that are an essential component of personal identity for many people.

How do people know if they are lesbian, gay or bisexual?

According to current scientific and professional understanding, the core attractions that form the basis for adult sexual orientation typically

emerge between middle childhood and early adolescence. These patterns of emotional, romantic and sexual attraction may arise without any prior sexual experience. People can be celibate and still know their sexual orientation – be it lesbian, gay, bisexual or heterosexual.

Different lesbian, gay and bisexual people have very different experiences regarding their sexual orientation. Some people know that they are lesbian, gay or bisexual for a long time before they actually pursue relationships with other people. Some people engage in sexual activity (with same-sex and/or other-sex partners) before assigning a clear label to their sexual orientation. Prejudice and discrimination make it difficult for many people to come to terms with their sexual orientation identities, so claiming a lesbian, gay or bisexual identity may be a slow process.

What causes a person to have a particular sexual orientation?

There is no consensus among scientists about the exact reasons that an individual develops a heterosexual, bisexual, gay or lesbian orientation. Although much research has examined the possible genetic, hormonal, developmental, social and cultural influences on sexual orientation, no findings have emerged that permit scientists to conclude that sexual orientation is determined by any particular factor or factors. Many think that nature and nurture both play complex roles; most people experience little or no sense of choice about their sexual orientation.

What role do prejudice and discrimination play in the lives of lesbian, gay and bisexual people?

Lesbian, gay and bisexual people in the United States encounter extensive prejudice, discrimination and violence because of their sexual orientation. Intense prejudice against lesbians, gay men and bisexual people was widespread throughout much of the 20th century. Public opinion studies over the 1970s, 1980s and 1990s routinely showed that, among large segments of the public, lesbian, gay and bisexual people were the

target of strongly held negative attitudes. More recently, public opinion has increasingly opposed sexual orientation discrimination, but expressions of hostility toward lesbians and gay men remain common in contemporary American society. Prejudice against bisexuals appears to exist at comparable levels. In fact, bisexual individuals may face discrimination from some lesbian and gay people as well as from heterosexual people.

Stereotypes persist even though they are not supported by evidence, and they are often used to excuse unequal treatment

---

Sexual orientation discrimination takes many forms. Severe anti-gay prejudice is reflected in the high rate of harassment and violence directed toward lesbian, gay and bisexual individuals in American society. Numerous surveys indicate that verbal harassment and abuse are nearly universal experiences among lesbian, gay and bisexual people. Also, discrimination against lesbian, gay and bisexual people in employment and housing appears to remain widespread.

The HIV/AIDS pandemic is another area in which prejudice and discrimination against lesbian, gay and bisexual people have had negative

effects. Early in the pandemic, the assumption that HIV/AIDS was a 'gay disease' contributed to the delay in addressing the massive social upheaval that AIDS would generate. Gay and bisexual men have been disproportionately affected by this disease. The association of HIV/AIDS with gay and bisexual men and the inaccurate belief some people held that all gay and bisexual men were infected served to further stigmatise lesbian, gay and bisexual people.

What is the psychological impact of prejudice and discrimination?

Prejudice and discrimination have social and personal impact. On the social level, prejudice and discrimination against lesbian, gay and bisexual people are reflected in the everyday stereotypes of members of these groups. These stereotypes persist even though they are not supported by evidence, and they are often used to excuse unequal treatment of lesbian, gay and bisexual people. For example, limitations on job opportunities, parenting and relationship recognition are often justified by stereotypical assumptions about lesbian, gay and bisexual people.

On an individual level, such prejudice and discrimination may also have negative consequences, especially if lesbian, gay and bisexual people attempt to conceal or deny their sexual orientation. Although many lesbians and gay men learn to cope with the social stigma against homosexuality, this pattern of prejudice can have

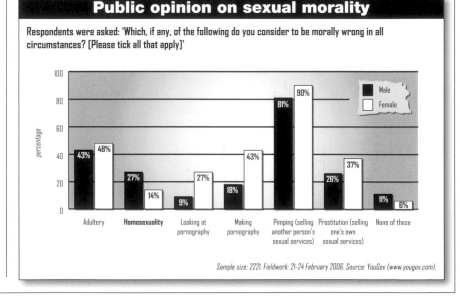

Public opinion on sexual morality

Respondents were asked: 'Which, if any, of the following do you consider to be morally wrong in all circumstances? [Please tick all that apply]'

Sample size: 2221. Fieldwork: 21-24 February 2006. Source: YouGov (www.yougov.com).

serious negative effects on health and well-being. Individuals and groups may have the impact of stigma reduced or worsened by other characteristics, such as race, ethnicity, religion or disability. Some lesbian, gay, and bisexual people may face less of a stigma. For others, race, sex, religion, disability or other characteristics may exacerbate the negative impact of prejudice and discrimination.

The widespread prejudice, discrimination and violence to which lesbians and gay men are often subjected are significant mental health concerns. Sexual prejudice, sexual orientation discrimination and anti-gay violence are major sources of stress for lesbian, gay and bisexual people. Although social support is crucial in coping with stress, anti-gay attitudes and discrimination may make it difficult for lesbian, gay and bisexual people to find such support.

Is homosexuality a mental disorder?

No, lesbian, gay and bisexual orientations are not disorders. Research has found no inherent association between any of these sexual orientations and psychopathology. Both heterosexual behaviour and homosexual behaviour are normal aspects of human sexuality. Both have been documented in many different cultures and historical eras. Despite the persistence of stereotypes that portray lesbian, gay and bisexual people as disturbed, several decades of research and clinical experience have led all mainstream medical and mental health organisations in this country to conclude that these orientations

represent normal forms of human experience. Lesbian, gay and bisexual relationships are normal forms of human bonding. Therefore, these mainstream organisations long ago abandoned classifications of homosexuality as a mental disorder.

What about therapy intended to change sexual orientation from gay to straight?

All major national mental health organisations have officially expressed concerns about therapies promoted to modify sexual orientation. To date, there has been no scientifically adequate research to show that therapy aimed at changing sexual orientation (sometimes called reparative or conversion therapy) is safe or effective. Furthermore, it seems likely that the promotion of change therapies reinforces stereotypes and contributes to a negative climate for lesbian, gay and bisexual persons. This appears to be especially likely for lesbian, gay and bisexual individuals who grow up in more conservative religious settings.

Helpful responses of a therapist treating an individual who is troubled about her or his same-sex attractions include helping that person actively cope with social prejudices against homosexuality, successfully resolve issues associated with and resulting from internal conflicts, and actively lead a happy and satisfying life. Mental health professional organisations call on their members to respect a person's (client's) right to self-determination; be sensitive to the client's race, culture, ethnicity, age, gender, gender identity, sexual orientation, religion, socio-economic status, language and disability status when working with

that client; and eliminate biases based on these factors.

What is 'coming out' and why is it important?

The phrase 'coming out' is used to refer to several aspects of lesbian, gay, and bisexual persons' experiences: self-awareness of same-sex attractions; the telling of one or a few people about these attractions; widespread disclosure of same-sex attractions; and identification with the lesbian, gay and bisexual community. Many people hesitate to come out because of the risks of meeting prejudice and discrimination. Some choose to keep their identity a secret; some choose to come out in limited circumstances; some decide to come out in very public ways.

Coming out is often an important psychological step for lesbian, gay and bisexual people. Research has shown that feeling positively about one's sexual orientation and integrating it into one's life fosters greater well-being and mental health. This integration often involves disclosing one's identity to others; it may also entail participating in the gay community. Being able to discuss one's sexual orientation with others also increases the availability of social support, which is crucial to mental health and psychological well-being. Like heterosexuals, lesbians, gay men and bisexual people benefit from being able to share their lives with and receive support from family, friends, and acquaintances. Thus, it is not surprising that lesbians and gay men who feel they must conceal their sexual orientation report more frequent mental health concerns than do lesbians and gay men who are more open; they may even have more physical health problems.

Exploring your sexuality

Straight, gay or bi, you don't have to label yourself immediately – or ever. However, exploring your feelings and accepting your sexuality is important

Get a grip

The most important thing is to be honest with your feelings and see where they take you. Sexuality is no easy ride; you have a whole host of emotions to get a grip of, not to mention the physical side of things.

Virtually everyone will have feelings for someone of the same sex at some stage in their life, this does not mean they have to rush out and buy a rainbow sticker for their car. It is just a natural part of sexual development. However, if these feelings are more frequent or long lasting then it may be more significant.

> **Virtually everyone will have feelings for someone of the same sex at some stage in their life**

Labels and stereotypes

Don't rush into giving yourself a label and coming out in public though. This is a very personal thing and you probably want to be comfortable with your feelings before broadcasting to your world.

Unfortunately some people can't accept any other sexual orientation to their own as being normal. They are mistaken in their thinking, and you must remember that you are not doing anything wrong or immoral. However, such prejudice can, understandably, be hard to take and you may be tempted to keep your sexuality quiet. While this may seem fine in the short term, do you really want to hide this side of you forever? Be true to yourself, you have every right to be comfortable with who you are.

Play safe

Just because you have decided your sexual orientation does not mean you have to get jiggy with the first person

you fancy. Give it time, and only get passionate when you feel ready.

Don't forget that it doesn't matter if you are gay, straight or bi – have safe sex to reduce the risk of pregnancy and getting any sexually transmitted diseases. It's also a good idea to know the law.

Find out more

You don't have to change yourself or your social life just because you have a different sexual preference to the rest of your mates. Life can tick on

as normal; however, it may help you to read books or articles written by or about people who have gone through the same thing as you.

You may also want to join a club or society run by gay people for gay people, it will give you the support of people who understand exactly what you are going through, and will be especially helpful if you feel uncomfortable discussing everything with your mates. Although it is worth remembering that you won't necessarily like every gay person you meet, just as you don't like every straight person you meet.

⇨ The above information is reprinted with kind permission from TheSite. Visit www.thesite.org for more information.

© TheSite

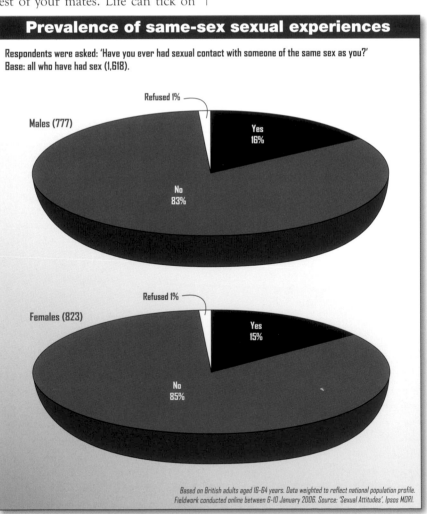

Prevalence of same-sex sexual experiences

Respondents were asked: 'Have you ever had sexual contact with someone of the same sex as you?' Base: all who have had sex (1,618).

Males (777)
- Refused 1%
- Yes 16%
- No 83%

Females (823)
- Refused 1%
- Yes 15%
- No 85%

Based on British adults aged 16-64 years. Data weighted to reflect national population profile. Fieldwork conducted online between 6-10 January 2006. Source: 'Sexual Attitudes', Ipsos MORI.

Just one in 100 tells researchers: I'm gay

Only one in 100 Britons would describe themselves as gay, according to the first government research into the nation's sexuality.

A further one in 100 would call themselves bisexual – but both groups are outnumbered by those who say they are unwilling to discuss their private life with Whitehall researchers.

In the survey, some people failed to understand the question and gave answers including 'female', 'normal', 'not active' and 'I am OK with my sexuality'.

Some interviewers declined to ask the question for fear of giving offence.

The Office for National Statistics, which carried out the poll of 4,000 people, admitted that its results were 'not a reliable estimate' of the homosexual population.

It said it would use the findings to develop a more accurate way of measuring.

By Ben Leapman, Home Affairs Correspondent

Ministers intend to introduce an annual count once the survey method has been improved. They say they need the information to plan public service provision more accurately.

However, the question will not be asked in the next census in 2011, for fear that it might deter some people from returning their forms.

Statisticians spent two years considering the precise wording of the sexuality question, which was asked as part of a larger survey about lifestyle. In the end, they asked it in two different ways, each bringing different results.

Overall, 94.4 per cent of people surveyed described themselves as heterosexual or 'straight'; one per cent said they were gay or lesbian; 0.9 per cent said they were bisexual; 0.6 per cent selected 'other'; and three per cent ticked the box for 'prefer not to say'.

No one objected to being asked, although interviewers reported that some sniggered or giggled out of amusement or embarrassment.

However, in 15 per cent of cases the interviewer failed to put the question, making the results difficult to interpret.

Overall, 94.4 per cent of people surveyed described themselves as heterosexual or 'straight'

Homosexual campaigners have claimed previously that as many as one in 10 of the population is gay. Ben Summerskill, the chief executive of the gay rights group Stonewall, believes the true figure to be about six per cent.

He backed the decision to carry out the survey, but said: 'There are sensible reasons for putting this question, but if you don't explain the reasons on the doorstep then people will get anxious and wonder why the man from the ministry is asking about their private life.'

In constructing the survey, statisticians grappled with the definition of homosexuality. Amanda Wilmot of the ONS said: 'Human beings do not always conform to a common standard.

'Those who are abstaining, or ignoring desires, or indeed those who are undecided or not yet "out", may not be able to classify themselves at all. One's desire, behaviour and self-identification might not always match.'

28 January 2008

© Telegraph Group Limited, London 2008

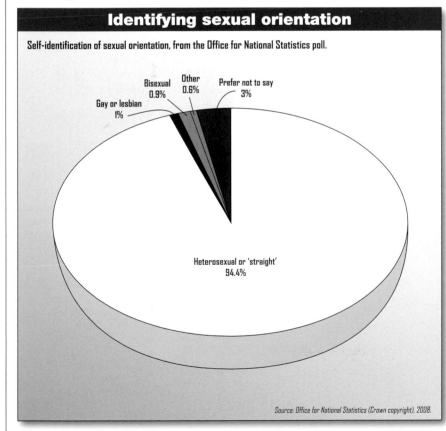

Identifying sexual orientation

Self-identification of sexual orientation, from the Office for National Statistics poll.

Bisexual 0.9%
Other 0.6%
Prefer not to say 3%
Gay or lesbian 1%
Heterosexual or 'straight' 94.4%

Source: Office for National Statistics (Crown copyright). 2008.

Theories

Information from Stonewall

Is there a 'gay gene'?

The term 'gay gene' refers to the gene that is thought to determine one's sexuality. Whether this gene actually exists is still subject to scientific debate.

Several studies have found there to be a genetic influence on the determining of one's sexuality – whether it be the levels of one's hormones or the size of certain parts of the brain (i.e. the corpus callosum or medulla oblongata). However, there is no conclusive proof that homosexuality is completely determined by genetic factors.

Studies suggest homosexuality to be a combination of environmental and biological factors

Eye colour, for example, is determined 100% by genetic factors, but height is only 90% determinable and is influenced by other factors such as nutrition. Because of this, height is said to be a 'multifactorial' trait. Studies of monozygotic (identical) twins revealed that if one brother is gay, there is a 52% chance that his twin is gay, suggesting a 70% attributable genetic factor (Bailey and Pillard, *A Genetic Story of Male Sexual Orientation*, 1990).

In the absence of conclusive proof as to whether homosexuality is completely biologically determined, the best answer is that the most current scientific studies suggest it to be a combination of environmental and biological factors. John Money, Emeritus Professor of Paediatrics at Johns Hopkins University, Maryland, USA, summarises the current scientific crux:

'Homosexuality is multi-varied. There is certainly a genetic component but there is not enough data to state that it is an exclusive influence. Hormones that affect the foetus play a part.'
Could You Be Gay for a Day? *Daily Express*, 7 July 1996.

It is certain that homosexuality is not a disorder of any kind and should not be treated as such

Even though popular medical opinion is not certain of the exact role that genetic factors play in determining one's sexual orientation, it is certain that homosexuality is not a disorder of any kind and should not be treated as such.

Homosexuality is not a mental illness

As early as the 1950s new medical research indicated that lesbians and gay men were not suffering from mental illness and could lead happy and productive lives. By the 1970s popular medical opinion reflected this research. Today there are few medical professionals that give the age-old 'mental illness' diagnosis for gay and lesbian patients.

The Royal College of Nursing agrees, stating in its 'Issues in Nursing Health Series' (10/97) that 'there is no intrinsic relationship between sexual orientation and mental illness. Homosexuality is not a mental disorder and there is no difference overall in the adjustment of people with same-sex or opposite-sex orientations.'

The American Psychiatric Association officially declassified homosexuality as a mental illness in 1974 but it wasn't until 1992 that the World Health Organisation followed suit.

Even though homosexuality is no longer classified as a mental illness, as the RCN states:
'There is a long legacy of an association between the two which continues to have an impact.'

As a result of this homophobia, there are a few doctors who still insist on 'reparative therapy' to combat same-sex attractions. This type of therapy is destructive, reinforcing self-hatred and contributing to unhappiness.

⇨ The above information is reprinted with kind permission from Stonewall. Visit www.stonewall.org.uk for more information.
© *Stonewall*

- THE THERAPY IS WORKING?

...HOMOPHOBIA IS DROPPING...

I am what I am and it's not a choice

After spending money and travelling the world in an effort to 'choose not to be gay', Toscano began to embrace his homosexuality and realised it is not a choice

Being gay myself, many folks consider me an expert on all things gay. Did Alexander the Great have a male lover? What does the Bible say about homosexuality? For my bay window, should I use lace or chintz curtains?

As a gay theatrical performance activist, the most common question I get is: 'how old are you?'

Such a rude question, but completely understandable because of my wild past including the 17-year quest to transform myself into a heterosexual with side trips to Zambia, England, and Ecuador plus a five-year marriage. They look at my fresh, young face and wonder 'how did you do all that?' I explain that I am a 42-year-old, non-smoking vegan who moisturizes (it is never too young to start!).

The second most common question I get is: 'do people choose to be gay?'

When someone is romantically and sexually attracted to someone of the same sex, is this nature or nurture? Genetics or a mere whim?

This is a scientific question, best left to scientists. No one knows for sure although researchers have amassed a body of evidence that points to biological factors leading to a same-sex orientation.

One recent study by J. Michael Bailey at Boston's Northeastern University revealed that among identical twin brothers, if one is gay, the other has a 52 per cent chance of being gay. (Fraternal twins show a 22 per cent chance while brothers who are not twins and do not share the same genetic code show only an 11 per cent chance of both being gay.) According to a 1997 Canadian study, Anthony Bogaert of Brock University in St Catharines discovered that the more brothers in a family, the higher the chance that the youngest ones will be gay.

By Peterson Toscano

No one has yet discovered the 'gay gene', but, then again, scientists have yet to discover a gene that causes some people to be left-handed.

Human sexuality is highly complex. We all start out in the womb as female, and then mom's body puts some of us through a hormonal rinse cycle, which turns us male. With such a complicated transition, who can say if all humans are 100 per cent male or female? Scientifically speaking we determine someone's sex according to many factors, not simply the bits between our legs.

Human sexuality is highly complex

But I stray into murky embryonic waters. Back to choice. Did I choose to be gay?

Yes, on 21 September 1972 in 2nd grade (age 7) I said to myself: 'Although most people treat gays like crap and only heterosexuality is represented and celebrated in my world, from this time forth I choose to like other boys instead of girls. Sure others will bully me, maybe even beat me up, but hey someone's got to be society's punching bag.'

Actually, no, I never chose to be gay. In fact, for nearly two decades I even tried choosing NOT to be gay.

Growing up I knew I was different from the other boys around me. When puberty hit and all my male friends went crazy for girls while I went crazy for my male friends, I understood the difference—I was gay, a homo, a queer, a faggot. From messages I heard on the playground, in the media and at church, I determined gays are sinful and abnormal. Instead I wanted to be a good boy.

So, at the age of 17 after giving my heart (and the rest of me) to Jesus, I embarked on a journey to straighten myself out. I spent 17 years and over $30,000 on three continents attempting to change or at least suppress my same-sex attractions. I discovered the Ex-Gay Movement, which promises that homosexuals can live gay-free lives. I reasoned that if being gay were a choice, a product of a dysfunctional upbringing in the midst of a lost and dying world, then surely with the power of God and the guidance of ex-gay ministers, I could 'un-choose' being gay or at least choose the right thing for a change.

No surprise, it didn't work. Change was not possible, at least not a change in sexual orientation. But through the years of trying I did change. I became suicidal, filled with shame and self-loathing. The ex-gay process left me depleted, discouraged and depressed. It caused emotional, psychological and spiritual harm.

No, I never chose my same-sex attractions. Also, after I came to my senses and came out of the closet, I did not choose to be 'gay'—to act gay according to the current standards and stereotypes presented in both the gay and straight media. Instead I chose to be authentic, to no longer demonise my sexuality, to integrate my faith with the rest of my life. I did choose to be a Christian, a Quaker, a vegan and an activist, but I never chose to be gay.

20 July 2007

⇨ The above information is reprinted with kind permission from the *New Statesman*. Visit www.newstatesman.com for more information.

When coming out goes wrong

Being up front with someone about your sexuality shouldn't be a big deal. Sadly, you can never be 100% sure of the outcome. If things haven't turned out as you hoped, here's how to handle it

Why come out?

Everyone has the right to be open about their sexuality. For those of you who do come out by telling friends and family that you're gay, lesbian or bisexual, it can be a big milestone in your life. If everything goes right, it means knowing that you can live your life freely and with nothing to hide. But if the response isn't what you had hoped for, the consequences can be hard to handle.

Your first feelings

Whether it's a parent, a sibling, friend or colleague who has reacted badly, you've got the hardest part out of the way by having the courage to confide in them. Common first emotions you can experience after telling people may range from shock and surprise, to a sense of disappointment and even humiliation. Nobody likes to feel like they're being judged, but in some ways this is what has happened. As a result, a sense of isolation and loss of confidence can quickly set in.

Coming to terms with what's happened

No matter how negatively those around you have responded, you are never alone. It's vital to remember that many people have faced a similar situation and found a way to deal with it that allows them to live life to the full. That's why it's so important to recognise help is always out there at any time.

Seeking help and support

If just one or two people have reacted badly, turn to other friends or family members for support. Ideally, they'll stand by you and give you a chance to talk. You may find that opening up about your feelings will help you to gain perspective. It'll also give you a chance to consider your next step.

Alternatively, if you don't feel you have anyone you can turn to, call the Lesbian and Gay Switchboard on 020 7837 7324. You can speak to a trained listener who will identify with what you're going through, and provide support and assurance – based on the experience of so many people before you – that you can get through this. Nothing has changed about you as an individual, after all. The only difference is some people have revealed their outlook on life to be very different from yours.

They can also put you in touch with local gay, lesbian and bisexual support groups in your area. This way, you can connect with like-minded people which will in turn provide you with the opportunity to be yourself.

Coming to terms with coming out

Once you're out, it's impossible to come back in. That's why the best advice to anyone considering being open about their sexuality is to be as sure as you can be that you're able to handle the consequences of your actions.

Nobody can predict what reaction you may receive, but reaching out for help and support will get you through the toughest of times. Ultimately, you should do what feels right. Some people may not agree, but let that be an issue for them and not you. Instead, build

on the support of friends and family who are willing to stand by you, and make every effort to talk to those who have come out in the past and can share their experiences.

Giving it time

Often, people react badly to news like this out of shock or surprise. Even if it exposes deep-seated views you didn't know they had, people can still change. Their outlook or opinions can be challenged by an episode such as this, or they may simply calm down and accept the situation. So long as you conduct yourself with dignity, they'll have to recognise that your sexuality hasn't changed who you are one bit. So keep an open mind right now, even if it feels as if relationships have broken down. Eventually, you may find that it brings a greater understanding of each other. You may even look back knowing you handled a difficult situation with sensitivity and self-respect, and came through feeling true to yourself.

➪ The above information is reprinted with kind permission from TheSite.org. Visit www.thesite.org for more information.

© TheSite.org

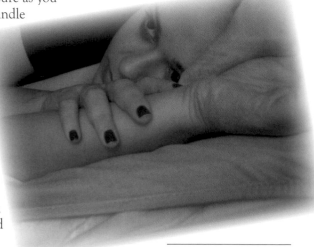

Parents of gay children

Reactions to coming out

By Nigel Cooper

She sobs uncontrollably. On several occasions, she tries to speak. She wants to say how she's feeling. It's been a full year since he told her, but she still can't talk about it. Her husband is telling the group how they found out, how they have been coping. She wonders how he has the strength. Even after a year, she still feels like the life has been drained out of her.

Your worst fear

Discovering a child is gay can be overwhelming and for many parents the initial shock can be devastating. Feelings of horror, disappointment and disbelief are all common. Some parents even feel bereaved, as if they have lost their child altogether.

Many parents just can't come to terms with the news of their child's sexuality – it's not what they had hoped for or dreamed of. It feels wrong, dirty and abnormal. Suddenly, the child they have always loved and cherished seems like a stranger.

Feelings of isolation, resentment and helplessness are common at this time and for most, the concept of having a gay child is so alien, they feel confused, angry, embarrassed and ashamed. Many parents find themselves worrying about what their neighbours, family and friends will think and because of these concerns, they feel alone, as if they have nobody to turn to.

HIV and AIDS

As the revelation sinks in, many parents begin to fear for their child's health. One of their first concerns is often HIV and AIDS, especially if they have a gay son. This is only natural – gay men are in a high-risk group for contracting the virus.

It's right to be concerned about your child's sexual health – but this fear should not necessarily go hand in hand with their sexuality. Avert, a UK-based HIV and AIDS charity, said that in 1999, a higher percentage of heterosexuals became infected with HIV than homosexuals – a trend that continues to this day.

Prejudice

Another key fear for parents is the disadvantages their son or daughter may face throughout their lives. Again, this is a valid concern – homosexuals do still face prejudice in the UK, but things are changing.

> Many of us have preconceived ideas of what gay men and women look, dress and sound like. But stereotypes are just that – stereotypes

Up until as recently as the last century, something as commonplace as left-handedness was frowned upon. Thankfully, this is no longer the case. Likewise, people's understanding of homosexuality is also improving.

Unknown territory

Many parents simply can't comprehend that their child is gay. The issue is too unfamiliar and they have no idea how to deal with it.

You shouldn't feel bad if you can't immediately accept your son or daughter's new identity. It is a difficult thing to come to terms with and it does take time.

However you feel initially, things can and do get easier. No matter how distressing it first seems, many parents find that in time, they learn not only to accept their child's orientation but also to embrace it.

Misconceptions

There are many misconceptions about homosexuality that can make life harder for the parents of gay children.

It's just a phase

One of the first things many parents think when their son or daughter comes out is that it is 'just a phase', or that their child is simply confused. However, it's unlikely that any child would say something so difficult and monumental if they weren't sure about it. The chances are, they have agonised over whether to come out for months or even years.

It can be cured

Homosexuality isn't an illness or a deficiency. In the past, treatments as harsh as electric shock treatment have been used in the attempt to 'cure' the 'condition'. Today, we know this isn't something that can, or needs to be, cured. It just is.

They don't look or act gay

Many of us have preconceived ideas of what gay men and women look, dress and sound like. But stereotypes surrounding homosexuality are just that – stereotypes. Homosexuals come in all different shapes and sizes, just like heterosexuals.

They are just trying to be trendy

Another common misconception is that teenagers are simply trying to be 'trendy' in some way. It is highly unlikely that any teenager will go through the trauma of coming out to his or her parents just because they think it's cool – more often than not, it isn't a pleasant experience. It's certainly not a trendy one. Would you describe yourself as gay if you weren't?

My child has been 'turned' or 'recruited'

Almost all gay children are brought up to be straight, yet turn out otherwise. Likewise, it is doubtful that a straight child could be 'turned' gay, even if someone was trying.

It is something I did

Nobody knows exactly why some people are gay, lesbian or bisexual but feelings of guilt are common. Many parents assume they somehow 'made' their child gay. As with the previous scenario, there is no evidence to support this notion.

Parent groups

Accepting that your child is gay and overcoming your learnt or inbuilt assumptions about homosexuality isn't going to happen overnight, so try not to feel bad if you can't discuss things openly with your son or daughter straight away. You will have to rebuild your relationship with your child and this might be a slow process – but you will get there. Bear in mind that coming out was probably a great ordeal for your child, too, and they may well have been asking for your support. But they should understand if this is difficult for you – especially if you're traumatised to the degree of the mother described earlier, who was so upset that she couldn't even speak without crying. A year after her son came out, she attended her first meeting of the Families and Friends of Lesbians and Gays (FFLAG). Slowly, she grew to understand her son's sexuality. Sue Allen, from the Bristol-based Families and Friends Group affiliated with FFLAG, said: 'After her first traumatic visit, she attended every meeting with her husband. Now, they work with FFLAG and have attended the London Mardi Gras with their son. They even joined the Age of Consent march on Parliament. They not only accept their son's homosexuality, they celebrate it.' FFLAG have local parent groups located throughout the UK aimed at helping the parents of homosexual children. Finding out that your child is gay needn't be the end of the world – it can be a new beginning.

⇨ The above information is copyright to Nigel Cooper and was first published by Channel 4. Visit www.channel4.com for more.

© Nigel Cooper

Bisexual

Information from the Terrence Higgins Trust

Bisexual is the word used to describe a person who is romantically and sexually attracted to both people of the opposite and of the same sex. Being bisexual does not mean that you have to like both boys and girls equally, or that you have to go out with both.

How do you know?

Some people may have always been attracted to both boys and girls, but for others it may be something that happens later on. It is not something you have to decide right away, or ever, as you may feel attracted to boys or girls at different times in your life. Remember it is your sexuality and up to you how you define it.

Denial

Some people think that people who describe themselves as bisexual are really gay but cannot admit this. This is not true; you can be attracted to both boys and girls and being bisexual is not the same as being gay. It is also not true that bisexual people are really straight but just experimenting.

Stereotypes

There are lots of stereotypes out there about being bisexual but it is important to realise that you do not have to change dramatically because of your sexual preference. After all you are still you, whoever you are attracted to. Some people think that if you are bisexual this means that you are promiscuous and are more likely to cheat on your partner. Neither of these things is true. How many partners someone has and whether they are unfaithful or not depends on the individual, not their sexual orientation.

Prejudice

Unfortunately people who are bisexual do sometimes experience prejudice from others because they think it is not normal and that you should decide whether you fancy men or women. This is called homophobia, and it is important to know that people who think this are wrong. More importantly, our society has systems in place to stop this sort of discrimination. Being bisexual is completely normal and you have the right to be who you are and have relationships with whoever you like.

Being bisexual does not mean that you have to like boys and girls equally

Meeting other people

Some people find joining a gay club or society really helpful, especially when they do not know many other bisexual people, as it can give them the opportunity to meet like-minded people. Growing up as a bisexual is not always easy and it can be very helpful to meet other people who understand any worries or difficulties you may be having. Of course that does not mean that you can only have gay or bi friends, or that your straight friends won't understand you.

⇨ Information from the Terrence Higgins Trust. Visit www.tht.org.uk for more information.

© Terrence Higgins Trust

Girls who like boys... and girls

Issues faced by bisexual people

By Melanie Ashby

During my teens, I went to an all-girls school, and never thought about sex. I had a female best friend, and we were close, nothing more. At university, I snogged a few blokes, then went out with a man at the age of 19. We slept together and it was fine.

> **Bisexuality is often thought of as a phase on the way to being gay, or as a form of sexual experimentation. It can be this but it can also be a mature sexual identity**

A couple of years later, I became friends with a woman who I knew was a lesbian and one night we fell into bed. I was freaked out, because she wanted me to say I was gay – but I wasn't sure. Our relationship didn't work out (thanks in part to my uncertainties), but it made me think a lot about my sexuality.

I figured I'd never been 'straight as a die' and this brought me out of myself. Living in gay-friendly Brighton – and meeting other women who identified as bisexual – was the key, and now I feel at ease with the idea of fancying, having sex with, and loving both men and women. The main thing is to 'come out' to yourself.

It's not just a phase

Society – parents, teachers, friends, whoever – tells us that there's straight, and then there's gay. It seems much neater that way. Bisexuality is often thought of as a phase on the way to being gay, or as a form of sexual experimentation. It can be this but it can also be a mature sexual identity

that you stick with through your whole life.

Some people (the famous psychoanalyst Sigmund Freud included) think that everyone is bisexual to some degree but that as we grow up, we are 'socialised' (convinced by society) to choose a love object of the opposite sex. In other words, we're brought up so we conform to the heterosexual or 'straight' norm. If we don't turn out to be nice and normal, we're gay, and that's becoming more acceptable too. Bisexuality, on the other hand, hasn't been so well understood, or tolerated.

I've fretted about what makes me fancy both men and women – but there's really no point; whether it's nurture, nature, gay genes or whatever, nobody has the complete answer to human sexuality. My idea is that there's straight and gay and there's a whole variety of sexualities in between. Some may simply fantasise,

some may try it out. Most importantly, your sexuality is your own: everyone has different things going on, whether you're gay, straight or whatever.

It's different for everyone. The way I work, I can have a gay day or have a straight day. Or sometimes I go on a woman-bent for a month, while the next minute I might be turned on by a particular bloke. Fantasies and dreams can go either way too. When it comes to getting involved, it depends on the person – not the person's gender.

Honesty's the best policy

The main thing is to be as honest with partners as you can. This does mean, though, that you have to deal with being 'queer' – and with all the stigmas attached. If you're afraid of having a same-sex experience, and you stay 'in the closet', it's not going to help your relationships. Experimentation is fine, as long as you make it clear what's in it for the other person.

Ultimately, you'll have to 'come out'. This can be a surprise for friends

who've known you as either straight or gay – but they get over it pretty quick. I haven't told my parents yet, which I'm not happy about. It's something I'm working up to.

Being bisexual doesn't mean you fancy everyone, and bisexuals aren't constantly 'up for it'

Sex-wise, being bisexual's a good deal for you and your partner... you can 'borrow' from sexual experiences with men and with women, learning how to give and get the best. However, as for people of all persuasions, remember safe sex, particularly if you're sleeping with different partners.

Finally, as you 'come out' you'll find others will tell you their experiences or fantasies. You may find yourself providing a counselling service for friends with bi urges. Respect those that insist they're fully straight or gay. That's the way they feel. But the way you feel is fine too.

Is it true?
Some people think...
Bisexuals have a ball, getting the best of both worlds, and a second-helping of sex life.
The truth is...
Being bisexual doesn't mean you fancy everyone, and bisexuals aren't constantly 'up for it'.
Some people think...
It's okay to be gay (they're born that way), but bisexuals choose to be perverse, they spread the HIV virus

with their indiscriminate sex lives, and they make a mockery of things such as marriage and the family.
The truth is...
You shouldn't pay heed to such nonsense. People like this always like to have a scapegoat.
Some people think...
I wouldn't touch them with a barge pole. Bisexuals aren't really dykes/gays/straight and they'll mess you about.

The truth is...
Being bisexual doesn't mean that you can't be monogamous, or that you will be looking 'the other way' all the time. That's just as likely or unlikely in any sort of relationship.

⇨ The above information is re-printed with kind permission from Melanie Ashby.

© Melanie Ashby

The wrong label?

Having doubts about whether it's basic curiosity or something more permanent? If you've labelled yourself as gay or straight this doesn't mean the label can't change

You came out young and were completely OK with it, but now you have feelings for someone of the opposite sex. What does this mean?
If you believe your attraction to this person goes beyond the boundaries of your sexuality, why not take the opportunity to ask yourself what these boundaries actually mean, and how they came to be imposed.

Gay or straight, it's just a category. A means of labelling yourself to conform to the way our society defines sex, gender and relationships. The trouble is our feelings and desires don't always sit so easily in this way, which can lead to a great deal of grief and confusion. Forget about the labels for a moment.

You're attracted to an individual, and the important thing is that you feel able to come to terms with these emotions. Try to have a heart-to-heart with the person in question, this will go some way to finding a positive outcome to this situation. Not just in terms of your feelings for him/her, but the bigger picture, too.

You've always considered yourself straight but you've recently been having feelings for people of the same sex...are you gay?
Your attraction to other guys/girls can mean as much or as little as you want. What's important is that you find a comfortable way to make sense of these feelings.

The fact is everyone comes to terms with their sexuality in different ways. Some people are sure they're gay from a very early age, while others go through periods of uncertainty or confuse same-sex admiration for sexual attraction. So don't fret about labelling yourself just yet. Ultimately, all that matters is that you're true to yourself.

⇨ The above information is reprinted with kind permission from TheSite. Visit www.thesite.org for more information.

© TheSite

Transgender

Information from the Terrence Higgins Trust

Gender in our society is split into masculine and feminine, and it is society – the people around us – that decides men and women should behave a certain way. Everyone has a gender identity, and this is separate and different from a person's sexuality. When people are described as transgender this suggests someone who feels that some aspect of the sex and gender they were born with does not fit who they feel they really are.

How do you know?

Some people say that they have felt like they are the 'wrong' gender, or that they are different from other people of the same gender, from a very young age, but for other people they may not be aware of how they feel until they start going through puberty.

All the same?

Everyone is an individual, and no two people feel exactly the same way. As a result, people explore their gender identity in different ways and may describe themselves using different terms. Below are explanations of a few of the most common terms people use:

Transgender
This is often used to describe anyone who does not feel they completely fit the gender and/or sex they were born with.

Transsexual
This is usually used to describe a person who feels that they were born the 'wrong' sex, and who identifies with and would like to be accepted as a member of the opposite sex. Many transsexuals want to change physically and do undergo sexual reassignment to change their bodies so that they are the sex they feel is right for them.

Transvestite or cross-dresser
These words describe a person who likes to dress in the clothes usually associated with someone of the opposite gender, such as a man liking to wear women's clothes, or a woman dressing as a man. There can be many reasons why people like to do this and it does not mean that they want to change gender or physically change their bodies.

Intergender or intersexual
These words describe a person who does not identify strongly as either male or female and who does not fit neatly into a typical masculine or feminine role. They can also be used to describe someone who naturally has both male and female physical characteristics.

Prejudice

Unfortunately transgendered people do experience prejudice from others, as many people do not understand why a person might feel that they have been born in the wrong body, or would like to wear the clothes usually worn by the opposite gender. This type of prejudice is called homophobia and can make people feel worried and vulnerable. More importantly, our society has systems in place to stop this sort of discrimination. The important thing to remember is that gender identity is not fixed and that everyone has the right to feel happy and comfortable and to be who they really feel they are.

Meeting other people

Some people find joining a gay club or society really helpful, especially when they do not know many other transsexual people, as it can give them the opportunity to meet like-minded people. Growing up as a transsexual is not always easy and it can be very helpful to meet other people who understand any worries or difficulties you may be having. Of course that does not mean that you can only have gay or bi friends, or that your straight friends won't understand you.

⇨ The above information is re-printed with kind permission from the Terrence Higgins Trust. Visit www.tht.org.uk for more information.

© Terrence Higgins Trust

Homophobia in the classroom

Information from About Equal Opportunities

Homosexuality is a sexual orientation characterised by an attraction to members of one's own sex. Gay men, for example, are attracted to men and lesbians are attracted to women. Many people are uncertain of their sexual orientations until they are adults, which makes the teen years a confusing and often frustrating time. Though school is meant to be a safe place for all, some teens are subjected to homophobia in the classroom. Both teachers and students can be responsible for homophobia, and bullying can take place whether an individual has come out or is simply suspected of a particular sexual orientation. Below are some suggestions for coping with homophobia in the classroom.

Understanding homophobia

Homophobia is the fear or hatred of homosexuals and homosexuality. Individuals who are homophobic fear or hate the fact that others are sexually attracted to members of their own sex. This fear can lead to behaviour that discriminates against homosexuals and consequently advantages heterosexuals. Such discrimination based on sexual orientation is illegal under the Equality Act (Sexual Orientation) Regulations 2007. This Act includes educational establishments, local education authorities and education authorities.

Homophobic bullying by other pupils

Homophobic bullying by other pupils can take many forms, from hurtful comments to physical attacks. In order to stop such bullying, students should first familiarise themselves with their school's anti-bullying policy. Students should also record instances of bullying in a diary, including what happened and who was involved, and tell a trusted adult about what is happening.

Any proof of bullying, such as defaced property or hurtful electronic communications, should be saved but online abuse (such as via text messages, emails, instant messages, websites or 'blogs') should not be responded to. When ready, the student and his or her parents should confront the school and make a formal complaint. While the bullying is being investigated the student should try to stay around others as bullies often begin their activities when their victim is alone. If a student is fearful for his or her personal safety then a self-defence class could be a good idea. However, no student should be encouraged to stand up to a bully alone and those who are being bullied should guard against becoming a bully themselves. Unfortunately some victims of bullying become so frustrated with the way they are being treated that they take it out on someone else, but this just perpetuates a cycle of bullying and hurts more people.

Homophobic bullying by teachers

It might be hard to imagine that teachers would stoop to bullying students, but sadly this can occur. Teachers may make degrading comments about a student, engage in unwanted or hostile physical contact with a student, make unwanted or suggestive sexual contact with a student, say inappropriate or lewd things to or about a student, or even suggest to a student that his or her grade depends on something other than his or her studies. If a student feels that they are being subjected to homophobic bullying by a teacher, the student should ask for a meeting with both the teacher and the department head. Parents may want to be at this meeting as well. If it is believed that nothing has come from the meeting then a formal complaint should be filed with the school. In the meantime, the student should discuss transfer options as a way of being removed from that teacher's class. It may not be fair that the student has to leave, but safety should be the first priority.

Educating others

Though it is not right, it is often left up to the individuals who recognise discrimination such as homophobia to educate others about why these practices are inappropriate. Often educating others about sexuality, homosexuality and sexual orientations is the first step in this process since it allows others to see that people of all sexual orientations are vibrant and have much to offer. If this is not enough to stop homophobia then educating others about the law and the consequences of discrimination may become necessary, as may getting the law involved in a specific case.

⇨ The above information is reprinted with kind permission from About Equal Opportunities. Visit www.aboutequalopportunities.co.uk for more information.

© *About Equal Opportunities*

Homophobic bullying

Executive summary of a report from Teachernet

Every child in every school has the right to learn free from the fear of bullying, whatever form that bullying may take. Everyone involved in a child's education needs to work together to ensure that this is the case.

Schools need to take an active approach to tackling all forms of bullying, including homophobic bullying. Schools should be taking action to prevent bullying behaviour, as well as responding to incidents when they occur. A preventative approach to bullying means that schools safeguard the welfare of their pupils. It also means that schools are playing their part to create a society in which people treat each other with respect. Schools know how to prevent and respond to bullying, and will already have strategies in place. Preventing and responding to homophobic bullying should be part of these existing strategies. This guidance helps with the specifics around homophobic bullying.

What is homophobic bullying?

Homophobic bullying occurs when bullying is motivated by a prejudice against lesbian, gay or bisexual (LGB) people.

Who experiences homophobic bullying?

⇨ Young people who are LGB.
⇨ Young people who are thought to be LGB.
⇨ Young people who are different in some way – they may not act like the other boys or girls.
⇨ Young people who have gay friends or family, or their parents/carers are gay.
⇨ Teachers, who may or may not be LGB.

Who does the bullying and why?

⇨ Anyone. Especially if they have not been told it's wrong.
⇨ They think that lesbian and gay people should be bullied, because they believe gay people are 'wrong'.
⇨ People who might be gay themselves, and are angry about that.
⇨ People who think 'boys should act like boys' and 'girls should act like girls'.
⇨ People who think gay people shouldn't have the same rights as heterosexual people and use this as justification for bullying.

Seven out of ten young lesbian and gay people say homophobic bullying affects their work

---

⇨ People who think gay parenting is wrong and pupils should be treated differently because of it.

Why should schools do anything about it?

Schools have a legal duty to ensure homophobic bullying is dealt with in schools. Under the Education and Inspections Act 2006, head teachers, with the advice and guidance of governors and the assistance of school staff, must identify and implement measures to promote good behaviour, respect for others and self-discipline amongst pupils, and to prevent all forms of bullying. This includes the prevention of homophobic bullying.

Homophobic bullying can have a negative impact on young people:
⇨ Bullying can also be linked to poor attendance with studies showing a high degree of absenteeism.
⇨ Seven out of ten young lesbian and gay people say homophobic bullying affects their work.
⇨ Low self-esteem, including the increased likelihood of self-harm and the contemplation of suicide.
⇨ Young people who experience homophobic bullying are unlikely to fulfil the objectives of Every Child Matters and Youth Matters.

How to recognise homophobic bullying

Homophobic bullying can be hard to identify because it may be going on in secret. Sometimes pupils may not want to tell anyone about it in case teachers/staff or other adults assume they are gay. A recent study found that three in five gay pupils never tell anyone (either at home or school) when they are being bullied. The fact that young people are particularly reluctant to tell is a distinctive aspect of homophobic bullying.

Generally, homophobic bullying looks like other sorts of bullying but in particular it can include:
⇨ Verbal abuse – including spreading rumours that someone is gay, suggesting that something or someone is inferior and so they are 'gay', e.g. 'you're such a gay boy!' or 'those trainers are so gay!'
⇨ Physical abuse – including hitting, punching, kicking, sexual assault and threatening behaviour.
⇨ Cyberbullying – using on-line spaces to spread rumours about someone or exclude them. Can also include text messaging, including video and picture messaging.

Can it happen in primary schools?

⇨ Yes. Pupils may not know what the words mean but can use homophobic language against others as a form of bullying.
⇨ They may bully a pupil who has gay parents/carers or family members.

21 September 2007

⇨ The above information is reprinted with kind permission from Teachernet. Visit www.teachernet.gov.uk for more information.

© Crown copyright

Sad to be gay

New guidance aims to end the rising tide of homophobic bullying – of pupils and teachers. Anna Bawden reports

Sam Clark, 19, first knew he was gay at the age of 10. Ever since, he has suffered from homophobic bullying. Things got worse after he came out at secondary school. 'I would be pushed over in the playground. Jokes were made openly in front of the teachers,' he says.

Clark is far from alone. A survey of 1,145 gay and lesbian secondary school pupils last summer by Stonewall found that almost two-thirds had been victims of homophobic bullying.

A survey of 1,145 gay and lesbian secondary school pupils found that almost two-thirds had been victims of homophobic bullying

---

The government wants this to change. New guidance is being launched tomorrow by the Department for Children, Schools and Families (DCSF) that aims to help schools prevent homophobic bullying and tackle it when it does occur.

'We wanted to make sure that within the overall anti-bullying guidance there was specific guidance on homophobic bullying,' says Ed Balls, the secretary for children, schools and families.

Stonewall's survey found that 41% of respondents reported physical attacks, 17% had received death threats and 12% had been sexually assaulted. Sarah, 14, was physically bullied at her school. 'Everyone knows and looks at me and threatens me and no one helps,' she told researchers. 'They push me in corridors and teachers have seen, but they act as if they haven't seen anything.'

'I have experienced bullying such as being verbally assaulted frequently, had scissors thrown at me, occasionally punched – sometimes directly in front of teachers,' says Kevin, 16.

Teachers join in

Astonishingly, far from clamping down on homophobic bullying, half the respondents said the teachers themselves had made homophobic remarks.

Emma Jones, 20, and Sophie Phillips, 18, say that when they got together at their sixth-form college in north Wales, they were discriminated against by some of their teachers. 'They would tell us off for inappropriate behaviour like hand-holding that would be tolerated among straight couples,' says Jones. In the classroom, Jones and Phillips say, the teachers drew attention away from them, effectively isolating them, and that comments from pupils were ignored.

'Homophobic language was regularly used in the classroom and the teacher never did anything,' says Phillips.

The DCSF recognises the need for action. 'I am proud the government and the department are being robust about this,' says Balls. It is the first time the government has formally addressed homophobic bullying. The guidance, written by Stonewall and Education Action Challenging Homophobia (Each), provides specific advice for governors, heads and senior management as well as teaching staff.

Balls says leadership has to start with the head and the governing body, but that everyone, including parents, pupils and teachers, has a responsibility to tackle homophobic behaviour.

'The guidance will give teachers more confidence to confront homophobic bullying in schools,' says Ben Summerskill, chief executive of Stonewall. 'It reiterates the importance of the need for the top level – from school management and governors – to get involved.'

Not tackling bullying can have dire consequences. Most young people who have been victims of homophobic bullying say their education suffered and many develop mental-health problems. Sam Thomas, 22, started getting bullied in year 7 because classmates thought he 'looked gay'. By year 9 he was being physically attacked in the playground and people threw things at him in class. 'I was getting depressed and would hide in the toilets,' he says. The depression caused by the bullying brought on bulimia. 'I didn't do very well at school because I was constantly skipping lessons,' he says.

The Education and Inspections Act 2006 requires schools to prevent all forms of bullying. The new guidance should be incorporated into schools' anti-bullying policies. It identifies 10 steps to address and prevent homophobic bullying. A priority is to ensure that schools' policies explicitly mention it. Balls says: 'It is our view that every school should have a clear policy on tackling all forms of bullying, including homophobic bullying.'

Kenny Frederick, the headteacher at George Green's school on the Isle of Dogs in London, says it is important to have integrated anti-bullying and equal opportunity policies that specifically mention homophobia. Posters put round the school make it clear that homophobic behaviour is not acceptable. If bullying does occur, action is swift. 'Every child has an entitlement to be respected for who they are,' she says.

She recommends that schools promote social cohesion and equality to specifically ensure gay, lesbian and bisexual pupils and teachers are not excluded, bullied or discriminated against.

Policies need to be followed up by action. The guidance provides advice on how to challenge homophobic language and how to deal with it robustly.

Thomas says schools need to tackle the use of the word 'gay'. 'It is misused as an alternative to "rubbish" or "not cool",' he says. 'If it was race, schools would crack down very quickly. The consequences are just as bad as racial bullying. It should not be pushed under the carpet.'

Chris Keates, general secretary of the Nasuwt union, says there is a hierarchy of bullying, and homophobic bullying comes very low down many teachers' priorities. 'It is considered to be part of growing up and normal playground taunts,' says Keates.

The new guidance recommends that if a pupil makes persistent remarks, they should be removed from the classroom and staff should talk in detail about why such language is unacceptable. Similarly, in severe circumstances, schools should consider permanent exclusion for physical bullying.

Much more needs to be done to prevent such bullying in the first place. Stonewall and Each advise encouraging positive role models. But Sue Sanders, co-chair of Schools Out, which campaigns against homophobia in education, says a big problem is that teachers find it hard to be out themselves. 'The government and local authorities need to celebrate the existence of lesbian, gay, bisexual and transgender teachers,' she says. 'If teachers don't feel safe to be out, how the hell will our kids?'

Bullied teachers

A surprising number of teachers experience bullying, too. According to figures from the Teacher Support Network, two-thirds of lesbian, gay, bisexual and transgender teachers and lecturers have experienced harassment and discrimination at work because of their sexual orientation; 71% of respondents experienced discrimination or harassment by their pupils, 46% by colleagues, 37% from their managers and 16% from parents.

Nasuwt says if teachers report being subject to homophobic bullying, the schools will often discourage them from taking it further. 'There's a tendency to say we need to keep this quiet,' says Keates. 'This means teachers are not confident to come out to their colleagues because they think it will be held against them.'

Prevention of bullying also means teaching pupils about sexuality.

'Being gay is just as normal as not being gay,' says Clark. 'This needs to be made clear.'

February is LGBT history month, which celebrates famous lesbian, gay, bisexual and transgender figures in history. This is an opportunity for everyone to learn more about the histories of lesbian, gay, bisexual and transgender people, says Sanders.

Stonewall and Each have provided lesson plans for how homophobia and sexuality might be addressed in the curriculum. And for teachers in rural areas, a project attempts to tackle the isolation that gay and lesbian young people experience in rural England. Ten young people from Herefordshire, Gloucestershire and south Wales have been selected from the project's online forum to make a short film about their experiences, which the organisers, Rural Media, hope to show at the Hay Festival. A DVD of the films, aimed at teachers and including lesson plans, will be sent to teachers in time for the next school year.

Tackling homophobic bullying is about respect. 'Gay [students] need to know that they are not alone, that it is alright to talk about it and that it is perfectly normal. The potential bullies need to know that homophobia will not be accepted, that all of us have an equal right to live lives free from bullying,' says Clark.

29 January 2008

© Guardian Newspapers Limited 2008

The school report

The experiences of young gay people in Britain's schools (2007)

Key findings

⇨ Homophobic bullying is almost endemic in Britain's schools. Almost two-thirds (65 per cent) of young lesbian, gay and bisexual pupils have experienced direct bullying. Seventy-five per cent of young gay people attending faith schools have experienced homophobic bullying.

⇨ Even if gay pupils are not directly experiencing bullying, they are learning in an environment where homophobic language and comments are commonplace. Ninety-eight per cent of young gay people hear the phrases 'that's so gay' or 'you're so gay' in school, and over four-fifths hear such comments often or frequently.

⇨ Ninety-seven per cent of pupils hear other insulting homophobic remarks, such as 'poof', 'dyke', 'rug-muncher', 'queer' and 'bender'. Over seven in ten gay pupils hear those phrases used often or frequently.

⇨ Less than a quarter (23 per cent) of young gay people have been told that homophobic bullying is wrong in their school. In schools that have said homophobic bullying is wrong, gay young people are 60 per cent more likely not to have been bullied.

⇨ Over half of lesbian and gay pupils don't feel able to be themselves at school. Thirty-five per cent of gay pupils do not feel safe or accepted at school.

⇨ The above information is reprinted with kind permission from Stonewall. Visit www.stonewall.org.uk for more information.

© Stonewall

Prevalence of homophobia in schools

Homophobic and sexist bullying is prevalent in majority of UK schools – ATL

Seventy per cent of teachers and lecturers report hearing terms such as gay, bitch, slag, poof, batty boy, queer and lezzie used in sexist or homophobic bullying in their school or college, according to an Association of Teachers and Lecturers (ATL) survey.

The findings come from a survey this summer of ATL members working in schools and colleges around the UK. They show the scale of the problem facing schools as they get £3 million from the Government to set up peer mentoring schemes to try to stamp out bullying in all its forms.

The survey reveals male pupils were the worst offenders when it came to name calling, but female pupils were also responsible for much of the verbal abuse. And in the majority of cases the victim was another pupil.

Teachers said the main reason for the name calling was a perceived lack of conforming to peer expectations,

the education union

followed by not belonging to a peer group.

ATL acting deputy general secretary, Martin Johnson, said: 'This survey gives an alarming picture of the extent of homophobic and sexist bullying in our schools and colleges. Schools have obviously still got a long way to go in combating these invidious types of bullying. We urge schools to use anti-bullying week to redouble their efforts to stamp out bullying and its root causes.

'Schools have a crucial role to play in challenging stereotypes and helping promote a society in which everyone is equally valued and respected, so it is

vital they play their part. We hope the Government's anti-bullying pilots are successful and that they are rolled out in the Further Education sector.'

He added: 'It is also important the Government and schools and colleges do not ignore bullying of staff, which is all too prevalent. We regularly get calls from teachers, lecturers and support staff who have been bullied by colleagues, pupils or parents. Frequently this is face-to-face bullying, but increasingly it is cyber-bullying by text or email or on the web. All schools and colleges should have a zero tolerance policy to bullying in its many forms, regardless of how it is done and who is the victim.'

16 November 2007

⇨ The above information is reprinted with kind permission from ATL, the education union. Visit www. askatl.org.uk for more information.
© ATL

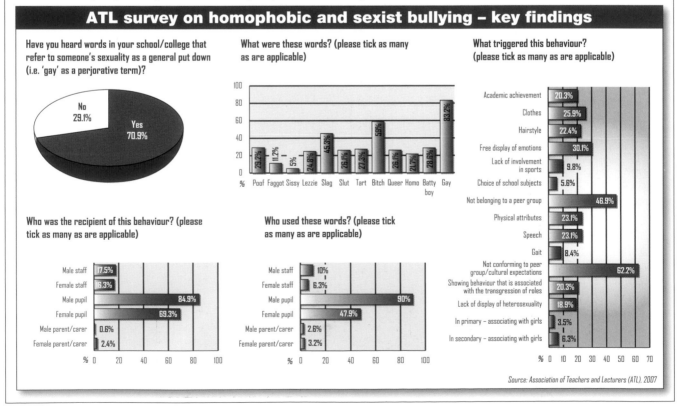

ATL survey on homophobic and sexist bullying – key findings

Have you heard words in your school/college that refer to someone's sexuality as a general put down (i.e. 'gay' as a perjorative term)?

No 29.1%
Yes 70.9%

What were these words? (please tick as many as are applicable)

	%
Poof	29.2%
Faggot	11.2%
Sissy	5%
Lezzie	24.8%
Slag	45.3%
Slut	28.1%
Tart	27.3%
Bitch	59%
Queer	25.5%
Homo	21.7%
Batty boy	28.8%
Gay	83.2%

What triggered this behaviour? (please tick as many as are applicable)

	%
Academic achievement	20.3%
Clothes	25.9%
Hairstyle	22.4%
Free display of emotions	30.1%
Lack of involvement in sports	9.8%
Choice of school subjects	5.6%
Not belonging to a peer group	46.9%
Physical attributes	23.1%
Speech	23.1%
Gait	8.4%
Not conforming to peer group/cultural expectations	62.2%
Showing behaviour that is associated with the transgression of roles	20.3%
Lack of display of heterosexuality	18.9%
In primary – associating with girls	3.5%
In secondary – associating with girls	6.3%

Who was the recipient of this behaviour? (please tick as many as are applicable)

	%
Male staff	17.5%
Female staff	16.3%
Male pupil	84.9%
Female pupil	69.3%
Male parent/carer	0.6%
Female parent/carer	2.4%

Who used these words? (please tick as many as are applicable)

	%
Male staff	10%
Female staff	6.3%
Male pupil	90%
Female pupil	47.9%
Male parent/carer	2.6%
Female parent/carer	3.2%

Source: Association of Teachers and Lecturers (ATL), 2007

The prince married a man, and lived happily ever after

Religious groups attack circulation of books raising gay issues among primary school pupils

A pilot scheme introducing books dealing with gay issues to children from the ages of four to 11 has just been launched in England's schools.

A pilot scheme introducing books dealing with gay issues to children from the ages of four to 11 has just been launched in England's schools

It is being argued that the books, one of which is a fairytale featuring a prince who turns down three princesses before falling in love and marrying a man, are necessary to make homosexuality seem normal to children. Fourteen schools and one local authority, backed by teaching unions and a government-funded organisation, are running the controversial scheme, which has been attacked by Christian groups.

Twenty years ago the publication of *Jenny Lives With Eric And Martin* for use in schools led to an angry public debate. In response the government passed Section 28, an amendment to the Local Government Act 1988, that prevented local authorities and, by extension, schools from 'promoting homosexuality' or its acceptability as a 'pretended family relationship'. The amendment was repealed in 2003 and this is the first large-scale attempt to put similar books back into the curriculum. Other books on the list of recommended texts for the schools, which have not been named, include a story about a spacegirl with two mothers and a baby penguin with

By Anushka Asthana,
Education Correspondent

two fathers. If successful, the scheme will be extended nationwide.

'The most important thing these books do is reflect reality for young children,' said Elizabeth Atkinson, director of the No Outsiders project that is being run by Sunderland and Exeter universities and the Institute of Education (IoE) in London. 'My background is in children's literature and I know how powerful it is in shaping social values and emotional development. What books do not say is as important as what they do.' Atkinson argued that leaving images of gay relationships out of children's books was 'silencing a social message', and could end up with children being bullied later in their school lives if they were gay or were perceived as gay. Atkinson and co-director Renee DePalma have received nearly £600,000 in funding from the Economic and Social Research Council and backing from the National Union of Teachers and General Teaching Council.

And they lived happily ever after

King & King
A queen wants her son to get married and become king. She arranges for a string of princesses to meet her son but he does not fall in love with any of them.

In the end it is one of the princesses' brothers who catches his eye. The princes get married and become two kings.

Spacegirl Pukes
A little girl who is about to set off on a space mission falls ill. Her two parents, mummy Loula and mummy Neenee, take her home to look after her but then they fall ill too. When she recovers, the spacegirl puts back on her suit and goes on an adventure to space.

And Tango Makes Three
Two male penguins, Roy and Silo, live in a New York zoo but feel left out when all their friends pair up. They spend all their time together until the zoo-keeper realises they must be in love. The zoo-keeper gives the couple an egg and Tango is born, the first penguin in the zoo with two daddies.

Waterstone's last week alerted its chain of shops to the titles that include *King & King*, *Asha's Mums* and *Spacegirl Pukes* and says it will start stocking them if the pilot is successful.

'Lots of fairy tales are about princes and princesses – why not two princes?' said Mark Jennett, who is training staff involved in the pilot from 14 schools and one local authority. '*King & King* is nothing to do with sex, it is about falling in love. *Cinderella* is not about sex – the problem comes not from kids but the nervousness of adults.' Jennett, who wrote *Stand Up For Us*, a government document on homophobia, said the work was 'cutting edge' and teachers were now more likely to challenge children if they used the word 'gay' in a negative way.

Critics say that the launch of the scheme shows that there is still a need for Section 28 type legislation. 'The predictions of those who said the repeal of Section 28 would result in the active promotion of homosexuality in schools are coming true,' said Simon Calvert, spokesman for the Christian Institute. 'Let's arrange a series of meetings around the country where parents of primary school children

can look at these books. The majority would be aghast.'

> ## It is being argued that the books are necessary to make homosexuality seem normal to children

Tahir Alam, education spokesman for the Muslim Council of Britain, agreed: 'This is not consistent with Islamic teachings and from our point of view many parents would be concerned.'

Other parents felt that children aged four and five were too young for the books. 'I don't know of many younger primary school children who would really understand what homosexuality is,' said Andy Hibberd, co-founder of the support group, the Parent Organisation, who has sons aged seven and nine. 'I don't have a problem with what happens between consenting adults, but I don't believe it needs to be forced on young children.'

⇨ This article first appeared in *The Observer*, 11 March 2007.
© Guardian Newspapers Limited 2007

Making babies the gay way

The last taboo

By Nigel Cooper

'Non-heterosexual couples lack the stable relationships that marriage guarantees. They lack the necessary balance of male and female role models. They threaten the sexual development and identities of children. Children are in danger of becoming little more than commodities, and their interests subordinated to the selfish desires of adults.'

> ## Current research shows the most important factor in a child's upbringing is love and stability

These are just a few of the common charges levied against gay parents, according to Weeks, Heaphy and Donovan in the book *Same Sex Intimacies*. In fact, the very idea of gay men and lesbians bringing up children seems to send shivers down the spine of middle England. Despite this, an increasing number

of lesbians and gay men are choosing to have children – and there is little evidence to support the often hysterical reaction they are faced with.

Current research shows the most important factor in a child's upbringing is love and stability, and that being a parent is about much more than gender or sexuality. It's about loving, educating and caring for a child in the best way possible,

whether you're male or female, gay or straight.

Common fears
There are a number of concerns for children raised by gay parents:
They will turn out to be gay
Almost all gay men and lesbians are brought up by heterosexuals in a heterosexual environment – but they don't turn out straight. There is no reason to suspect the opposite is true for the children of gay parents. It isn't only common sense that debunks this myth.

Jeffrey Weeks, Professor of Sociology and Dean of Humanities at London South Bank University, explains, 'Studies in both the UK and the US have shown that children brought up by gay parents are no more or less likely to be gay or straight than children brought up by heterosexual parents. The only difference seems to be that the children of lesbians and gay men aren't as hung up about sexual distinctions.'

Opponents of gay parenting cite bullying as reason enough to exclude homosexuals from the role of carer, often forgetting that homophobia is at the core of this problem, not gay parents themselves

---

They will lack balanced male/ female role models

A similar accusation is often aimed at single parents, too – but the fact is, many single parents and couples, gay or straight, have close family and friends of both sexes that play an active part in the lives of their children, providing an array of role models. Professor Weeks said, 'All children need to be aware of emotional behaviours, both masculine and feminine, but there is no reason to suggest the children of gay couples will miss out on this.'

There also seems to be a bigger problem in society with the thought of men bringing up children, as women are traditionally the primary care givers in a family situation. The fact that women are generally excellent parents doesn't exclude men from this role, however. I doubt anyone would suggest that Bob Geldof was an unfit parent because of his gender.

They will be bullied

It would be naive to suggest that the children of gay men and lesbians are not going to encounter some problems because of their parents'

sexuality. These issues may range from the child's own embarrassment (especially in the early teenage years) to outright bullying and non-acceptance from their peer group. Lisa Saffron from Pink Parents said, 'There is bullying. Despite a lot of progress, we still live in a homophobic society.'

If Britain really does care about its children, perhaps it should be supporting the different family units that are a growing part of modern society

---

But it is also true that children face bullying for a number of other reasons, whether they have gay parents or not – and the modern family bears little resemblance to the nuclear family idealised in the 1950s. Children today are brought up in a variety of situations, from single-parent households to stepfamilies. Some are raised by grandparents and others by non-related carers. Professor Weeks said, 'Just to pick out gay parents to depict the changing family dynamic is wrong – it is part of a much wider shift.' Any one of

these situations might leave a child open to bullying or abuse, as might any number of other factors, such as their weight, sporting ability or the clothes they wear.

Opponents of gay parenting cite bullying as reason enough to exclude homosexuals from the role of carer, often forgetting that homophobia is at the core of this problem, not gay parents themselves, or their children. It is also possible that, because of their own experiences, gay parents may be more capable than heterosexual couples of helping their children deal with any bullying or prejudice they do encounter.

Lisa Saffron said, 'Gay men and lesbians know how much bullying can impact on self-esteem and they don't want to see their children suffer it. We have developed strategies to deal with homophobia and can try to help our children deal with it, too.'

Parent skills

Being gay doesn't automatically make someone a bad parent, nor is it a demonic infection, ready to invade Britain's children. Parenting isn't about gender or sexual preference; it's about how much time you invest in your child and the love and stability you show them. It's about putting them first – and there is nothing to suggest that gay men and women are any less capable of doing this than heterosexuals.

Lisa Saffron said, 'Your parenting style and ability depends on how you were parented, the child-rearing culture of which you are a part and your belief system and values. It has nothing to do with your sexuality.'

There also seems to be a bigger problem in society with the thought of men bringing up children, as women are traditionally the primary care givers in a family situation

---

If Britain really does care about its children, perhaps it should be supporting the different family units that are a growing part of modern society rather than condemning them for not fitting in to an ever-changing definition of what constitutes a family.

⇨ The above information is copyright to Nigel Cooper and was first published by Channel 4. Visit www.channel4.com for more.

© *Nigel Cooper*

Gay adoption

The First Post presents the arguments for and against

Arguments for

⇨ Many gay couples – certainly those offering themselves as adoptive parents – form relationships that are more stable than many heterosexual marriages, thus giving adopted children a secure emotional home.

⇨ In an era when many children are raised by single parents – with proven disadvantages such as lower educational achievements and poor behaviour – gay couples offer adopted children two full-time parents.

⇨ Lesbian couples are permitted to have children through artificial insemination. The record is that such couples provide loving homes and raise well-balanced children.

⇨ Barring gay men and lesbians from becoming 'parents' is discrimination, based on sexual orientation, which would not be acceptable in other contexts such as employment.

⇨ There is a shortage of adoptive parents. The 'family', whether gay or straight, is better than the foster-care system.

Arguments against

⇨ To grow up to be well-balanced adults, children need role models of both sexes. Boys without fathers under-achieve, especially since there are now fewer male teachers in primary schools.

⇨ We are a 'Christian' country – even if few go to church, our values remain based on Christian teaching. Two parents are axiomatic – 'Honour thy father and mother', invokes the Fifth Commandment.

⇨ Children raised by gay parents are offered only one partnership model and are therefore (some argue) more likely to be gay.

⇨ If Roman Catholic adoption agencies close rather than allow gay couples to adopt, the number of adopted children will decline, leaving more in the unsatisfactory care system.

⇨ Some areas of life cannot be legislated for and must be left to individual conscience. A sufficiently large minority simply find gay parenting 'wrong'; the practice therefore should not be enforced on all.

24 January 2007

⇨ The above information is reprinted with kind permission from *The First Post*, the daily online news magazine. Visit www.thefirstpost.co.uk for more information.

© *First Post*

Homosexuality in the media: is the press good?

Information from Gay Youth Corner

By Sacha Coward

In 1960 the first ever kiss between a same-sex couple was televised on the family favourite British soap opera, *Coronation Street*. This was a breakthrough for a society where Kenneth Williams' style of closeted high-camp was the closest television ever got to touching on the issue of homosexuality. Jump to now, every show from *Dawson's Creek* to *The Archers* has had its token gay relationship, indeed you'd be hard put to find a show without gay undertones. This must be a good thing... right?

People can no longer escape the fact of homosexuality when it's everywhere they look, from their favourite soap to the magazines they read in dentist waiting rooms. But is all of the mass portrayal of homosexuality entirely beneficial – have we really broken down boundaries or just built new ones?

Homosexuality is no longer portrayed on television as something dirty and immoral: but more than that, the gay lifestyle is no longer merely put up with. Shows like *Sex and the City*, *Queer Eye for the Straight Guy*, and *Will and Grace* have shown it's popular; homosexuality sells! What could be better to promote an edgy new television programme than a saucy sharp-tongued gender-bending host, or a pink-tank-top-wielding fashion icon? It is because of their selling power – their popularity – that we have an endless parade of gay stereotypes, entertaining and inoffensive to the masses, but ultimately damaging. To argue that these crowd-pleasing caricatures are helping to make the media more representative would be ridiculous: these aren't real people merely cartoon characters. Maybe we haven't really moved on as far as we would like to think we have.

Even though your television set may be awash with gay men making bitchy comments and mincing about, the old taboos are still very much present. Let's face it, while gays may sell, gay sex categorically does not: people will happily enjoy watching *Will and Grace* but show them a gay sex scene and instead you've got thousands of disgusted viewers on your hands. Anal sex is still not commercially viable for the masses, and so it is cleaned up. This active repackaging of homosexuality is happening all the time. On the big screen, Hollywood blockbuster *Brokeback Mountain* may be making waves, but just take a look at this specially produced poster [the image which originally appeared here cannot be reproduced for copyright reasons. The image was of a promotional poster for the film *Brokeback Mountain* which showed one character with his wife and child, although the actual focus of the film was on his relationship with another man. It can be viewed at www.thegyc.com/images/stories/brokebackposter.jpg].

Funny that when it comes to the stereotype-affirming pink-tank-top-wielding glitterati the majority are happy enough to tune in, but when shown a gritty realistic relationship between two men, sex and all, the majority shrink away. Looking at this image you'd think you were going to see a nice romcom, not perhaps the most controversial genre-subverting film of the year. In conclusion, homosexuality sells, but only when it is served up lukewarm, minus the sex, and fitted into a people-friendly stereotype. Examples of this are everywhere; *Queer Eye* depicts homosexuals as human Barbie dolls (manicurists and personal shop assistants) and *Sex and the City* shows us primped-up gay guys whose only purpose is to be fashionable accessories to successful young arty women. What a depressing set of role models for young gay society, and what a pathetic example of homosexuality for society as a whole. While admittedly it is unfair to say that all media portrayal of homosexuality is equally biased (with television shows like *Queer as Folk* giving a far more accurate and brazen account of the gay scene), these are few and far between.

This level of publicity doesn't mean that being gay is necessarily accepted; it is just popular like a new trend or a fashion statement, and only then when it is sterilised and wrapped in a bright pink ribbon. This portrayal is not only demeaning and patronising, it is dangerous. Can a change from complete disapproval of the gay lifestyle to approval of a censored version, a version hung up on labels where gay isn't just a sexuality, it's a franchise, a defining personality trait, be classed as a real step forward? While it is important to get homosexuality well and truly out of the closet, it must also be remembered that not all publicity is good publicity.
26 March 2006

Disappearing act

In the 1990s, gay storylines were all the rage in mainstream television; now they are all but non-existent. Campaigners accuse broadcasters of failing to reflect modern Britain

By Stephen Armstrong

Remember that lesbian kiss on *Brookside*? And the first episode of the groundbreaking gay drama *Queer as Folk*? There was a period, in the 1990s, when television seemed to be ahead of the curve with its brave and humane treatment of homosexuality. A few years later, however, there's barely a gay storyline to be found on all of Britain's major channels. The relationship between broadcasters and gay campaigning organisations is on the rocks, with the BBC standing accused of being the worst offender.

The gay campaigning organisation Stonewall recently monitored prime-time programming on BBC1 and BBC2 over two weeks and found that, during 168 hours of programming, there were just six minutes that portrayed lesbian and gay lives in a positive manner, as opposed to 32 minutes involving negative terms or contexts. More than half of all the gay references were jokes about sexually predatory or camp and effeminate gay men. 'Gay and lesbian licence payers provide the BBC with £200m every year,' says Stonewall's chief executive, Ben Summerskill. 'For that, we get "the only gay in the village" on *Little*

Britain and a hint that Captain Jack in *Doctor Who* might sleep with men as well as women. Even heterosexual respondents in our focus groups who didn't know any gay people said they expected to meet lifestyles they were unfamiliar with on the BBC. It's just not happening.'

The relationship between the BBC and gay campaigners was poisoned in 2005 when the Radio 1 DJ Chris Moyles used the word 'gay' in a derogatory sense during his live breakfast show. Following a complaint, the BBC board of governors ruled that Moyles was 'not being homophobic in his use of the word', as it was 'often now used to mean "lame" or "rubbish".' According to Summerskill, the corporation is in denial about the depth of its institutional homophobia. 'If you talk to the corporation about representation of gay and lesbian people they won't even admit there's a problem,' he says.

The *New Statesman* took Summerskill's comments to the BBC and made a formal request for an interview

to deal with each criticism in turn. The BBC chose instead to issue the following statement: 'We believe there is a great deal of richness and diversity in BBC output across television, radio and online. We are committed to finding ways of reflecting the audience's daily lives in our programmes, but we feel the notion that gay men and lesbians only receive value for money from the licence fee through seeing direct representation of gay life is misconceived. Gay men and lesbians do of course enjoy our output across the board.'

There was a period, in the 1990s, when television seemed to be ahead of the curve with its brave and humane treatment of homosexuality

For Summerskill, this is not an adequate defence. 'We've been talking to the BBC for two years about this and [the response] shows they haven't listened to a word,' he says. 'It confirms the trite notion that gay people should be grateful that the *Ten O'Clock News* is on at all – and shouldn't cause a fuss if they're simply never covered by it. I guess it is emblematic of the problems at the heart of the BBC in understanding this diverse and complex nation.'

Other mainstream broadcasters are much better at representing the gay community, Stonewall argues. '*Coronation Street* [on ITV] and *Hollyoaks* [on Channel 4] both have strong gay characters with storylines that aren't just about coming out,' says Ben Summerskill. 'Rather counter-intuitively, ITV seems to be doing

---

40 years of screen queens

1970s Mr Humphries in the BBC comedy *Are You Being Served?* became a gay icon, though – as John Inman, the actor who played Humphries, observed – his sexuality was never explicitly stated. The character was less popular with some gay rights groups, which objected to his stereotypically mincing walk and high-pitched catchphrase: 'I'm free!'

1980s The long-running Australian drama *Prisoner: Cell Block H* featured several lesbian characters in admirably nuanced roles. It became a cult hit across the world.

1990s The first lesbian kiss on UK prime-time television was between Beth Jordache, played by Anna Friel, and Margaret Clemence, played by Nicola Stephenson, on *Brookside* in 1993. It caused so much controversy that it was cut from the omnibus edition later in the week.

2000s *Little Britain* introduced Daffyd, 'the only gay in the village', played by Matt Lucas. Daffyd obsessively accuses bystanders of homophobia, in a role strongly criticised by gay rights campaigners.

---

its best by putting a gay war-hero son and his boyfriend in Victoria Wood's *Housewife 49* and updating the Miss Marple mysteries to include lesbian characters.

'Even Channel 5 usually includes a selection of salacious gay references in its usual smut.'

There are, indeed, honourable exceptions to the general decline in television coverage of homosexuality. Most notably this year, Channel 4 has programmed a season to coincide with the 40th anniversary of the decriminalisation of homosexual acts between consenting gay men. The season's centrepiece, *Clapham Junction*, is a drama inspired by the murder of Jody Dobrowski, manager of a Camden comedy club, on Clapham Common, south London, in 2005. The season includes three other programmes: *A Very British Sex Scandal*, a docudrama about the controversial 1954 trial of Lord Montagu of Beaulieu and Peter Wildeblood which prompted the change in legislation; *How Gay Sex Changed the World*, a documentary about the progress of the gay rights movement over the past 40 years; and *Queer As Old Folk*, a look at the present-day lives of gay men who came of age when homosexuality was still illegal.

Beautifully shot and tightly scripted, *Clapham Junction* revolves around five separate stories of gay life in London over a hot summer weekend. Starring Paul Nicholls and Samantha Bond, it is scripted by Kevin Elyot, who is best known for his 1994 play *My Night With Reg*, one of the first stage productions to address the spread of HIV and Aids in the UK. Elyot explains that one of the aims of *Clapham Junction* was to show that the past 40 years have not been a time of unadulterated success for the gay rights movement. 'While there seems to be a greater acceptance of gays in society – consent equality, civil partnerships, higher media visibility – homophobic violence has not disappeared,' he says. 'Bigotry is still bubbling just below the surface, and sometimes in the most surprising quarters.'

Ironically, it seems that one of these quarters is television. The Channel 4 season is the only programming across all five main channels this year to deal with gay and lesbian issues. The channel scrapped its post of gay and lesbian commissioning editor at the turn of the century, and insists that ghetto programming is not the solution. However, in mainstream dramas, gay characters have been becoming less and less common since the late 1990s. Richard Bevan, TV reviewer for the lesbian and gay website Rainbow Network, argues that positive gay characters on television are especially important for children struggling with their sexuality.

'We've moved on since the Seventies, when the only portrayal of homosexuality was John Inman and the occasional tranny in a *Sweeney* episode,' says Bevan. 'There were no role models for gay people, particularly young gay people, living in an era when homosexuality was seen as deviant, seedy, unwholesome or something to pity. No kid at school in those days would ever own up to being queer, because they didn't want to be associated with the kind of creatures that were meant to represent homosexuality on screen.'

Bevan acknowledges that most broadcasters are more likely to include gay characters in soap operas today than they were in the past. He points out, however, that many of the strongest gay characters are actually from US imports – which indicates that the religious right does not have as tight a hold on the chief US regulator, the Federal Communications Commission, as we might have feared. Gay characters in American programmes broadcast on British television in the past few years include Will and Jack in *Will and Grace*, David and Keith in *Six Feet Under*, Andrew Van de Kamp in *Desperate Housewives*, Marc in *Ugly Betty*, Dr Kerry Weaver in *ER* and, most recently, Kevin in *Brothers and Sisters*. There are also secondary characters in such shows as *The Sopranos* and *My Name is Earl*.

Damon Romine, entertainment media director for the US Gay and Lesbian Alliance Against Defamation, is pessimistic about the prospects for commissions. 'When you look at the American broadcast networks, gay and lesbian characters represent slightly more than one per cent of all the characters on TV,' he says. 'The networks really have failed to capitalise on the visibility and discussion about our lives that has gone on for the past couple of years. *Brokeback Mountain*, *Capote* and *Transamerica* found audiences anxious to see our stories. *Will and Grace* showed that a series with gay characters can be popular, yet the networks really have not developed any series to capitalise on this success. The ABC channel, with *Desperate Housewives*, *Ugly Betty* and *Brothers and Sisters*, is the only exception.'

Thus, as Channel 4 begins its season, an event that should be a reason for celebration is actually a cause for concern. According to government figures, roughly six per cent of the UK's population is gay. But gay people are still woefully under-represented across all national TV channels, and most seriously on the BBC, which should be leading the way.

19 July 2007

⇨ The above information is reprinted with kind permission from the *New Statesman*. Visit www.newstatesman.com for more information.

Civil Partnership Act 2004

Frequently asked questions. Information from the Women and Equality Unit

The Civil Partnership Act 2004 covers the whole of the UK, though the different legal frameworks in Scotland and Northern Ireland may mean there are differences in the way the legislation is applied. The information given in these FAQs reflects the law on civil partnership as it applies in England and Wales.

Enquiries about civil partnership in Scotland should be referred to:

Scottish Executive
Justice Department
Civil Law Division
St Andrews House
Edinburgh EH1 3DG
Tel: 0131 244 3581
Website: www.scotland.gov.uk/
Topics/Justice/Civil/18313/12657
Email: civilpartnershipregistration@
scotland.gsi.gov.uk

Enquiries about civil partnership in Northern Ireland should be referred to:

The Office of Law Reform
Lancashire House
Belfast BT2 8AA
Northern Ireland
Tel: 028 90 542900
Website: www.olrni.gov.uk
Email: info@olrni.gov.uk

General information about civil partnership

When will my partner and I be able to register a civil partnership?
The Civil Partnership Act 2004 came into force on 5 December 2005 and the first civil partnerships were registered in England and Wales under the standard procedure on 21 December 2005.

How does civil partnership differ from marriage?
Civil partnership is a completely new legal relationship, exclusively for same-sex couples, distinct from marriage.

The Government has sought to give civil partners parity of treatment with spouses, as far as is possible, in the rights and responsibilities that flow from forming a civil partnership.

There are a small number of differences between civil partnership and marriage: for example, a civil partnership is registered when the second civil partner signs the relevant document, a civil marriage is registered when the couple exchange spoken words. Opposite-sex couples can opt for a religious or civil marriage ceremony as they choose, whereas formation of a civil partnership will be an exclusively civil procedure.

> **Civil partnership is a completely new legal relationship, exclusively for same-sex couples, distinct from marriage**

Who is eligible?
The couple must both be of the same sex, not already be in a civil partnership or marriage, be 16 years of age or older, and not be within the prohibited degrees of relationship (i.e closely related).

In England and Wales and Northern Ireland, people who are aged 16 and 17 will have to obtain the written consent of their parent(s) or legal guardian(s) before registering a civil partnership. In Scotland individuals aged 16 or over will be able to register their partnership without the need for parental consent. (This is also the rule, in Scotland, for opposite-sex couples who marry.)

The prohibited degrees of relationship can be found in Schedule 1 to the Civil Partnership Act for England and Wales, Schedule 10 for Scotland and Schedule 12 for Northern Ireland. These Schedules list the people who, due to the closeness of their relationship with each other, are prohibited from registering a civil partnership with each other or, in certain cases, who are prohibited from registering a civil partnership with each other unless certain conditions are met.

How many people do you expect to register civil partnerships?
The Government expects between 11,000 and 22,000 people to be in a civil partnership by 2010. The full take-up assumptions are available in the final Regulatory Impact Assessment published by the DTI at http://www.dti.gov.uk/access/ria/index.htm#equality

Registering a civil partnership
What arrangements can I make for my civil partnership?
If you want to register a civil partnership, you will be able to give formal notice of your intention to do so from 5 December 2005. You should contact your local register office to make a booking and find out what arrangements you can make.

Where can I register my civil partnership?

The range of places you can register your civil partnership will be broadly similar to those available for civil marriage. Every local authority is required to provide a facility for the registration of a civil partnership. It will also be possible to register a civil partnership at approved premises such as hotels and stately homes etc. Any premises that are presently approved for marriage will also be approved for civil partnership registrations until the current approval is renewed or expires. After 5 December 2005, premises are approved for hosting both civil partnerships and marriages. Premises can choose to host marriages or civil partnerships or both.

It is possible for a civil partnership to be registered at the residence of someone who is housebound, detained or seriously ill and not expected to recover.

What formal requirements have to be met before registration can take place?

You and your partner will need to each give notice in the area(s) where you have lived for at least seven days. When you give notice, you will be asked to state where you wish the civil partnership registration to take place.

If a civil partnership is to be registered outside of the area you live in, you and your partner will still need to give notice in the area(s) where you live. When you each give notice, you will be asked to give the date and place where the civil partnership registration is to take place so these details will need to have been first agreed with the local authority where the registration is going to take place and the venue.
Example:
If you live in Brighton and your partner lives in Eastbourne, but you want to register a civil partnership in a country house hotel in Kent, you will give notice to your local register office in Brighton and your partner at Eastbourne register office. When you give this notice, you will both have to be able to give the date and the place where the civil partnership is to be registered, which means that you will have to have arranged this already with the venue and the Kent registration authority.

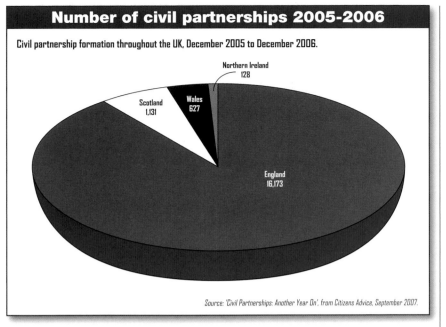

Number of civil partnerships 2005-2006

Civil partnership formation throughout the UK, December 2005 to December 2006.

Northern Ireland 128
Scotland 1,131
Wales 627
England 16,173

Source: 'Civil Partnerships: Another Year On', from Citizens Advice, September 2007.

What is the waiting period for civil partnership?

There is a 15-day waiting period once each person has given notice of intention to register, before the civil partnership can be registered.
Example:
You give notice on 1 July and your partner gives notice on 3 July. The first date the registration can take place is on or after 19 July, which is 15 clear days from the date of the second notice. The notice is valid until 1 July the following year, which is 12 months from the date of the first notice.

It is possible to reduce the 15-day waiting period in exceptional circumstances where there are compelling reasons to do so.

There is also a procedure to allow couples to register a civil partnership quickly in the cases of former spouses, one of whom has changed gender under the provisions of the Gender Recognition Act 2004.

What time of day can a civil partnership be registered?

Civil partnerships can only be registered between 8am and 6pm (as is the case for marriage). However, where one of the couple is seriously ill and not expected to recover, then the civil partnership may be registered at any time.

What information will be made public about my civil partnership?

When you give notice of your intention to register a civil partnership, details from the notice will be available in a register office for public inspection (as for marriage) but the details will not include the address of you or your partner.

It is important that these details are publicly available during the 15-day waiting period, to allow for objections to be made, just as is the case for marriage.

What happens at a civil partnership registration?

A civil partnership is registered once the couple has signed the civil partnership document in the presence of a registrar and two witnesses.

If they wish to do so, the couple can speak to each other the words printed on the document: 'I declare that I know of no legal reason why we may not register as each other's civil partner. I understand that on signing this document we will be forming a civil partnership with each other.'

Civil partnership registration is an entirely secular process, and the Civil Partnership Act prevents any religious service from taking place during the statutory steps leading to the formation of a civil partnership.

Can we have a ceremony?

Yes, you can arrange a ceremony in addition to the signing of the legal documentation if you wish, but a ceremony is not required under the Act. It is up to you to decide. Most local authorities in England and Wales will offer a ceremony but there are other organisations who also offer ceremonies. The Association of Registrars and Celebratory Services, after consultation with members of the gay community, has drawn up a model ceremony which can be seen at http://www.arcs.uk.com/index. php?page=cps

What will the whole process cost?

The fees for registering a civil partnership are as follows:

➪ for giving notice in advance of forming a civil partnership: £30.00 per person.

➪ for registering a civil partnership at a register office: £40.00

➪ for registering a civil partnership at an approved premises: there will be the cost for attendance by a civil partnership registrar as set by the registration authority and a further charge is likely to be made by the owners of the building for the use of the premises.

➪ civil partnership certificate (on the day of registration): £3.50.

➪ civil partnership certificate (additional copies): £7.

Can I use Welsh?

Yes, all forms used in Wales in connection with civil partnerships will be printed in Welsh and English. It will be possible for these forms to be completed in English or in Welsh and English as for marriage.

Can we change our names after registering a civil partnership?

After registering a civil partnership, some people might want to change their surname to that of their partner's, or a couple may choose to hyphenate their names. Government departments and agencies such as the Passport Agency and the DVLA will accept civil partnership certificates in the same way that they accept marriage certificates as evidence for changing names.

Dissolving a civil partnership

How will dissolution proceedings work?

Registering as civil partners is a serious commitment, because a civil partnership ends only on formal dissolution or annulment, or on the death of one of the parties. The process for dissolution will be court-based. The person applying for the partnership to be dissolved will have to provide evidence that the civil partnership has broken down irretrievably.

The dissolution process will begin with an application to the court in the form required by the court rules for civil partnership proceedings.

In order to prove irretrievable breakdown it will be necessary to provide evidence of one or more of the following facts to support the application for dissolution:

➪ Unreasonable behaviour, that is behaviour such that the applicant cannot reasonably be expected to live with their civil partner;

➪ Separation for two years, where the other civil partner consents to a dissolution order being made;

➪ Separation for five years, where the other civil partner does not consent to a dissolution order being made;

➪ That the other civil partner has deserted the applicant for a period of two years prior to the application. The court will be required to inquire as far as is possible into the facts alleged by the applicant and into any facts alleged by their civil partner. If the court is satisfied on the evidence that the civil partnership has broken down irretrievably, a dissolution order can be granted.

Tax, pensions and workplace benefits

Will I have equal survivor pension rights as a civil partner, i.e. the same as for widowers?

Civil partners will be able to accrue survivor pensions in public service schemes and contracted-out pension schemes from 1988.

The Department for Work and Pensions has just made amendments to the contracting-out rules to ensure that pension schemes provide survivor benefits for civil partners on the basis of deceased members' rights accrued from 6 April 1988, to treat them on a par with widowers. For full details of the changes go to: www.dwp.gov.uk/consultations/2005/index.asp

How will civil partnership affect tax?

For tax purposes civil partners will be treated the same as married couples. Tax charges and reliefs and anti-avoidance rules apply equally to married couples and civil partners, and those treated as such. Information

is available from local tax offices and the HMRC website www.hmrc.gov.uk

What about council tax?

Civil partners and same-sex couples living together as if they were civil partners will be treated in the same way as married couples and opposite-sex couples living together as if they were married. Some of the changes take effect from 1 April 2006.

Civil partners and people living together as civil partners will be jointly and severally liable for council tax in the same way that married couples and people living together as husband and wife are jointly and severally liable. This means that both partners in a same-sex couple are responsible for seeing that the bill is paid.

For tax purposes civil partners will be treated the same as married couples

---

As of 1 April 2006, changes will be brought into effect to council tax discounts, exemptions, and to the way that council tax is recovered. See this link for further details: http://www.local.odpm.gov.uk/finance/ctax/ctil/5ctiloct05.pdf

For general information on council tax, contact your relevant local authority or go to http://www.local.odpm.gov.uk/finance/ctax/ctaxbillguide.pdf

Will I receive the same workplace benefits as a married employee?

The Employment Equality (Sexual Orientation) Regulations 2003 have been amended to require that civil partners and spouses should be treated in the same way in relation to workplace benefits.

➪ The above information is reprinted with kind permission from the Department for Trade and Industry's Women and Equality Unit. Visit www.womenandequalityunit.gov.uk for more information.

© Crown copyright

Are civil partnerships really civil?

A new report 'Another Year On' from Citizens Advice investigates the impact and unforeseen consequences of the Civil Partnership Act 2004

The report shows:
⇨ Same-sex couples are being inadvertently 'outed' owing to the generic nature of corporate and bank forms.
⇨ People are struggling with the ambiguity of language surrounding civil partnerships and don't know how to refer to their circumstance in social situations.

As part of Citizens Advice commitment to helping all clients solve their money, legal and other problems, and to influence policy makers, the national charity is proud to launch the report 'Another Year On' which explores the impact of the Civil Partnership Act 2004 and the potential needs of advice-seeking clients.

The launch coincides with the second anniversary of the civil partnership legislation, which allowed same-sex couples the right to the same legal responsibilities and rights as married couples. The report reveals that while many same-sex couples, who are in or who are planning civil partnerships, find there are many benefits to civil partnership, and welcome it, there are still potential emotional, financial and social costs that come with this radical social change.

Some key issues have been identified by the report. Localised evidence suggests people are struggling with the ambiguity of language surrounding civil partnerships, and don't know how to refer to their circumstance in social situations, due to a lack of conversational terms that are equivalent to the terms of the traditional marriage.

The research also found that gay and lesbian couples who had formed a civil partnership were forced into revealing their sexual orientation, in situations which required disclosure of marital or partnership status.

Citizens Advice is calling for all banks and businesses to use the straightforward solution to amend pro forma to have a single category of 'married/civil partner' leaving the sexual orientation of any respondents unspecified.

David Harker, Chief Executive of Citizens Advice, said,

'What consistently amazes me is the amount of policy work and research that goes on throughout the Citizens Advice network, alongside our key role of advising clients. Salford CAB have shown great ingenuity in thinking about the role of civil partnerships, and offering evidence-based suggestions that help people.'
5 December 2007

⇨ The above information is reprinted with kind permission from Citizens Advice. Visit www.citizensadvice.org.uk for more information.

© Citizens Advice

Civil partnerships fall by 55%

Information from the Local Government Association

The number of civil partnerships fell by more than half last year compared to the previous year, according to a new survey by the Local Government Association.

Thousands of gay couples rushed to tie the knot when the Civil Partnership Act came into force on 5 December 2005, allowing them to obtain legal recognition of their relationship.

But new figures obtained by the LGA have uncovered an average 55 per cent drop in numbers in 2007, compared with the previous year.

A total of 40 councils around the country reported between a 31 per cent and 90 per cent drop in the number of ceremonies. Most councils reported more gay men than women getting hitched.

Only one council, Barnsley, reported an increase in same-sex civil partnerships, of 14 per cent.

A typical council which experienced a high demand for civil partnerships is Wandsworth, south-west London, where 231 same-sex couples (192 male and 39 female) tied the knot up to the end of 2006 and 100 (64 males and 36 female) did so in 2007. This represents a 57 per cent decrease.

Others include:
⇨ Devon – 226 couples (123 male and 103 female) up to the end of 2006 compared to 93 (47 male and 46 female) in 2007, a 59 per cent drop.
⇨ Kent – 329 couples in 2006,

compared to 168 in 2007, a drop of 49 per cent.

⇨ Essex – 230 couples (121 male and 109 female) by the end of 2006, compared to 112 (51 male and 61 female) in 2007, a 52 per cent decrease.

⇨ Blackpool – 178 couples (109 male and 67 female) up to the end of 2006 compared to 77 (44 male and 33 female) in 2007, a 57 per cent drop.

One council reported that most ceremonies were cancelled at the last minute. Wigan and Leigh received 94 notices in 2005/2006 but only conducted 31 ceremonies, and 55 notices in 2007, but only 17 couples went through with ceremonies.

Unlike the national trend, more gay females than males married in Blackburn, North East Lincolnshire and St Helens.

The smallest drop in gay marriages was in Barnet, north London (31 per cent), and the largest in Bracknell Forest (90 per cent).

Notes

According to the Office for National Statistics, there were 18,059 civil partnerships formed in the UK between December 2005 and the end of December 2006. A total of 16,173 took place in England with 1,131 in Scotland, 627 in Wales and 128 in Northern Ireland. Almost 2,000 partnerships were formed in December 2005. On average, 1,600 partnerships were formed each month between January and March 2006, falling to 1,500 between April and September and 800 between October and December.

More men than women formed civil partnerships. In 2006, 60 per cent of all civil partners were male. *5 February 2008*

⇨ The above information is reprinted with kind permission from the Local Government Association. Visit www. lga.gov.uk for more information.
© Local Government Association

The European Convention and Court of Human Rights

Information from Stonewall

European Convention on Human Rights

One of the most significant achievements of the Council of Europe is the European Convention on Human Rights signed in 1950. The Convention provides a set of rights for each individual and places an obligation on the countries who have signed the Convention to guarantee these rights to each individual within their jurisdiction. The following articles of the Convention are particularly relevant to lesbians, gay men and bisexuals:

⇨ Article 3 – No one shall be subjected to torture or to inhuman or degrading treatment or punishment.

⇨ Article 8 – Everyone has the right to respect for his private and family life, his home and correspondence.

⇨ Article 10 – Everyone has the right to freedom of expression. The right shall include freedom to hold opinion and to receive and impart information and ideas without interference by public authority and regardless of frontiers.

⇨ Article 14 – The enjoyment of the rights and freedoms set forth in this Convention shall be secured without discrimination on any grounds such as sex, race, colour, language, religion, political or other opinion, national or social origin, association with a national minority, property, birth or other status.

None of the articles refer specifically to the rights of lesbians, gay men and bisexuals since the creators of the Convention did not have these rights in mind. However, the judges of the European Court of Human Rights in their case-law regarded the Convention as a 'living instrument' and demonstrated that Convention rights can be interpreted widely according to the social and attitudinal developments and changes in the member states of the Council of Europe to include lesbian, gay and bisexual rights.

Until recently, lesbians, gay men and bisexuals could not use the protection of Article 14 of the Convention against the discrimination they faced. This was because the creators of the Convention designed the Article in such a way that it did not specify sexuality and could only be used in conjunction with other articles of the Convention.

This situation improved when Protocol 12 of the European Convention on Human Rights was agreed in 2000. This created an independent right not to be discriminated against and placed a duty on public authorities not to discriminate. Article 1 of Protocol 12 reads:

'1. The enjoyment of any right set forth by law shall be secured without discrimination on any ground such as sex, race, colour, language, religion, political or other opinion, national or social origin, association with a national minority, property, birth or other status.

2. No one shall be discriminated against by any public authority on any grounds such mentioned in paragraph 1.'

Although sexual orientation is again not mentioned among the prohibited grounds of discrimination, the case-law of the European Court of Human Rights established that sexual orientation can be included in 'other status' in the list of prohibited discrimination. Unfortunately, the UK has neither signed nor ratified this protocol and lesbians, gay men and bisexuals in the UK cannot directly rely on its provisions.

European Court of Human Rights

The European Court of Human Rights is a mechanism that allows individuals in Europe to use the protection of the European Convention on Human Rights in practice. If an individual feels that their rights as guaranteed in the Convention have been violated by the state, they can complain to the European Court of Human Rights, having first used all the available judicial avenues of that state.

The Court considers the application and if the issue falls within the remit of the Convention, the Court examines the case and delivers its judgement. Judgements of the Court are legally binding for the state against which a complaint was launched.

Until a couple of years ago, there was also a European Commission of Human Rights. The Commission carried out the original sifting for the European Court of Human Rights and scanned all incoming complaints. The Commission decided which cases were forwarded to the Court for judgement and which were declared inadmissible. Now the Commission no longer exists and the Court alone considers which cases should be examined and which do not fall within the remit of the Convention.

⇨ The above information is reprinted with kind permission from Stonewall. Visit www.stonewall.org.uk for more.
© *Stonewall*

Gay adoption in Europe

European Court of Human Rights says lesbian, gay and bisexual individuals are eligible to adopt children

Today the Grand Chamber of the European Court of Human Rights delivered its judgement in a case of *E.B. v France* and said that exclusion of individuals from the application process for adoption of children simply because of their sexual orientation is discriminatory and is in breach of the European Convention of Human Rights.

Ms E.B. is a lesbian nursery school teacher who has been living with another woman since 1990. She applied for approval as a possible adoptive parent in February 1998, but her application was rejected, essentially because of her sexual orientation. In June 2002, the highest administrative court in France upheld the rejection of her application.

ILGA-Europe, FIDH (Fédération Internationale des Ligues des Droits de l'Homme), APGL (Association des Parents et futurs Parents Gays et Lesbiens) and the BAAF (British Association for Adoption and Fostering) were granted permission to take part in the proceedings as third parties.

In 2002 in the very similar case of *Fretté v France*, the European Court of Human Rights ruled by four votes to three that the exclusion of a gay man from the application process for adoption of children, because of his sexual orientation, did not violate the Convention (but only one judge in the majority considered the exclusion justifiable; the other three rejected the case on technical grounds).

Patricia Prendiville, Executive Director of ILGA-Europe, said:

'We welcome today's judgement of the European Court of Human Rights. This is a significant change in the Court's approach towards and interpretation of the rights of LGBT people under the European Convention on Human Rights. Today the Court firmly established a principle that administrative officials cannot discriminate against an individual on the basis of her/his sexual orientation in the process of applying to adopt a child. This builds on the Court's judgments in *Smith & Grady v United Kingdom* (1999), that LGBT people must be allowed to serve in the armed forces, and *Mouta v Portugal* (1999), that the sexual orientation of a parent is irrelevant when determining who should have custody of a child.

'Until today France permitted administrative officials to exclude openly lesbian, gay and bisexual individuals from applying to adopt children. The European Court of Human Rights has decided that such a practice is discriminatory and violates the European Convention on Human Rights.

'No one has an automatic right to adopt a child. But what the European Court of Human Rights said today is that European countries can no longer justify exclusion of lesbian, gay and bisexual individuals from applying for a child adoption. The Court has established the principle that ILGA-Europe has long fought for – each individual should be

---

No one has an automatic right to adopt a child

---

treated equally on the basis of their individual merits as a potential parent when applying to adopt a child. The sexual orientation of the applicant is irrelevant and cannot be used to exclude them from the possibility of adopting a child. It is in the best interest of children in Europe and outside Europe that no potential adoptive parent be excluded from consideration for an irrelevant and discriminatory reason.'
22 January 2008

⇨ The above information is reprinted with kind permission from ILGA-Europe. Visit www.ilga-europe. org for more information.
© *ILGA-Europe*

Church loses opt-out fight over gay adoptions

By George Jones, Political Editor

Roman Catholic adoption agencies yesterday lost their battle to opt out of new laws banning discrimination against homosexual couples when Tony Blair announced that there would be 'no exemptions' for faith-based groups.

The Prime Minister said in a statement that the new rules would not come into force until the end of 2008. Until then there would be a 'statutory duty' for religious agencies to refer gay couples to other agencies.

Earlier, David Cameron risked a split with Tory traditionalists by announcing that he was against allowing Catholic adoption agencies to opt out of new laws banning discrimination against gay couples. He called for a compromise that would give the Catholic agencies time to find a way of dealing with the regulations – possibly by developing twinning arrangements with other adoption services.

Last week the leader of Catholics in England and Wales, Cardinal Cormac Murphy-O'Connor, warned that the agencies would close rather than accept rules that required them to hand over babies to gay couples.

Last night, the Roman Catholic Church expressed its 'deep disappointment' with the decision but the cardinal issued a conciliatory statement saying there was now an 'urgent task' to reach a 'new consensus' over how the rights of religious organisations could be upheld.

He hinted that a face-saving compromise might still be worked out to preserve the Catholic adoption agencies in some form.

Downing Street said Mr Blair's statement reflected the Government's position and Labour MPs – unlike Conservative members – would not be given a free vote when the new regulations were put before Parliament next month.

Ruth Kelly, the Communities Secretary, a prominent Catholic who had been pressing for an exemption for the Church, said the announcement was a 'breakthrough' that should be 'welcomed by everyone'.

But the decision that Catholic agencies – which say they have a religious objection to placing children with gay couples – must fall into line is a defeat for both Miss Kelly and the Prime Minister.

Their attempt to secure an opt-out for the Catholic Church had caused a deep rift in the Cabinet, with senior ministers, including John Reid, Lord Falconer, Alan Johnson and Peter Hain, insisting that there must be no exemptions.

Mr Blair said he believed that ministers had found a 'way through' that prevented discrimination and protected children's interests, which all 'reasonable people' would be able to accept.

There was 'no place in society for discrimination', and he supported the right of gay couples to apply to adopt.

'And that way there can be no exemptions for faith-based adoption agencies offering public-funded services from regulations that prevent discrimination.'

The regulations under the Equality Act, which forbid schools, businesses and other agencies from refusing services to people on the grounds of sexual orientation, would be brought forward by the Government 'shortly'.

Mr Blair said there would be a transitional period before the new rules came fully into force at the end of 2008 for existing adoption agencies. During this period, it would be a statutory duty for any adoption agency that did not process applications from same-sex couples to refer them to another agency.

Miss Kelly said the approach represented 'a positive breakthrough in eliminating discrimination' while recognising the need for a practical approach that ensured the most vulnerable children were found loving homes.

'We now have a workable solution,' she said. 'At the end of the day, we all know that there is a wide range of potential adoptive parents out there, including lesbians and gay men, who can provide a loving home for children.'

Mr Johnson said the announcement was the right outcome for all concerned because it put the interests of children first. 'We reject discrimination in all its forms, particularly when that deprives our most vulnerable children of a stable, loving and secure home,' he said.

Mr Cameron's backing for gay adoptions puts him at odds with his shadow home secretary, David Davis, who has said he would 'almost definitely' vote for an exemption for the Catholic agencies. The Tory leader promised his MPs a free vote, saying it was an issue of conscience.

Mr Cameron told BBC Radio 4's *Today* programme: 'I shall vote for the regulations because it is right to have clear rules against discrimination.'

Cardinal Murphy-O'Connor said in his statement: 'We are, of course, deeply disappointed that no exemption will be granted to our agencies on the grounds of widely-held religious conviction and conscience.

'We note and welcome, however, the Government's desire that the excellent work of our agencies is not lost.'

31 January 2007

The right to equal treatment: parental rights

Information from Liberty

Parental responsibility

Biological parents

The biological mother of a child, and the biological father if married to the mother at the time of birth, automatically gain parental responsibility. Since 1 December 2003, a non-married father registered on the child's birth certificate will also automatically gain parental responsibility. Otherwise a non-married father can only obtain parental responsibility by agreement with the mother, or a court order. This may affect gay fathers who have had children in a previous relationship, or have fathered a child through sperm donation.

On termination of the relationship, a biological parent can apply to the courts for a residence order (custody) or for a contact order (access). In determining such orders the court will consider what is in the child's best interests. A refusal to provide access or custody on the grounds of sexual orientation will be a breach of Article 8 (right to respect for personal and family life) and Article 14 (prohibition on discrimination) of the European Convention on Human Rights.

LIBERTY

PROTECTING CIVIL LIBERTIES
PROMOTING HUMAN RIGHTS

Civil partners who are not biological parents

Under the Civil Partnership Act 2004 ('CPA'), when you enter a civil partnership with a person who has a child, you will become the step-parent on the same basis as a married non-biological parent. This confers no real legal status and the biological parents remain the legal parents. However, it does enable you to more easily acquire parental responsibility in the same way as married step-parents under the Adoption and Children Act 2002. This enables you to obtain parental responsibility either by consent of those biological parents who have parental responsibility or a court order. Alternatively you can apply to adopt the child (a process which could sever the links with one or both biological parents). There is

no requirement for a civil partner adopting their partner's child to go through an agency or to live with the child for six months. Civil partners may also apply to become a guardian of the child; however, this status is likely to be revoked if the civil partnership is terminated.

Civil partners are under a duty to provide maintenance for each other and any children of the civil partnership.

Non-civil partners who are not biological parents

A non-civil partner who is not a biological parent cannot become a step-parent of their partner's child. They can only obtain parental responsibility by obtaining a court order or applying to adopt the child on the same basis as non-married couples.

Fertility treatment

It is lawful for lesbian women to receive donor insemination or for gay men to use a surrogate mother. However, currently private clinics are not obliged to offer this service, and there is no entitlement to NHS treatment. In December 2006, the government published its review of the Human Fertilisation and Embryology Act. This includes proposals to remove the 'need for a father' when considering 'the welfare of the child' when determining whether to provide fertility treatment. The proposed amendment recognises same-sex civil partnerships and relationships on the same basis as married and non-married heterosexual relationships.

In addition, under the Sexual Orientation Regulations 2007 it is unlawful for both private and NHS clinics to refuse treatment to lesbian and gay men on the same basis as heterosexual men and women, since this would constitute discrimination in the provision of goods, facilities

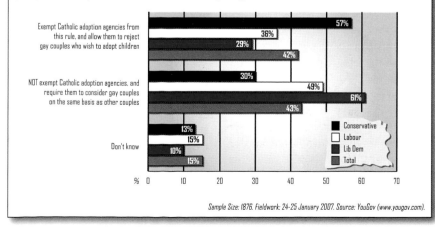

The gay adoption debate

Respondents were asked: 'Parliament recently passed the Equality Act, which gives people the right to be treated equally in a variety of circumstances. These include the right of gay couples to adopt children. Catholic adoption agencies wish to be exempt from this particular rule. They say that adoption by gay couples is against religious principles. What do you think Parliament should do?'. By voting intention.

Exempt Catholic adoption agencies from this rule, and allow them to reject gay couples who wish to adopt children — 57%, 36%, 29%, 42%

NOT exempt Catholic adoption agencies, and require them to consider gay couples on the same basis as other couples — 30%, 49%, 61%, 43%

Don't know — 13%, 15%, 10%, 15%

Conservative / Labour / Lib Dem / Total

Sample Size: 1876. Fieldwork: 24-25 January 2007. Source: YouGov (www.yougov.com).

Support for LGBT legal protection

Almost nine in ten Britons support new legal protections in major nationwide survey of public attitudes to gay people

⇨ *73% would not mind if their child's teacher was gay.*

⇨ *80% would not mind if a relative was gay.*

⇨ *88% would not mind if member of royal family was gay.*

Major new polling commissioned by Stonewall has found that the vast majority of Britons, 85%, support the 2007 Sexual Orientation Regulations, newly-introduced legal protections for gay people. Similar numbers would be happy if a relative, their boss or a footballer in the team they support (92%) was gay, the Living Together survey established. The vast majority believe that further steps should be taken to tackle homophobia by government, workplaces, schools and the media.

YouGov sampled 2,009 respondents from across Britain to gauge public opinion towards gay people. While a significant majority expressed high levels of tolerance, 73 per cent said that anti-gay prejudice needed addressing. Eighty-nine per cent support a new offence of incitement to hatred on the grounds of sexual orientation, to match existing protections against incitement to racial hatred.

Eighty-five per cent of adults also support the government's new Sexual Orientation Regulations, fiercely opposed by some religious leaders earlier this year, which make it unlawful to refuse gay people services such as healthcare or hotel rooms. But while religion is identified as a significant cause of anti-gay prejudice, the number of people of faith supporting gay equality is almost as high as the figure in the wider population.

The survey also found that:
⇨ More than a third of adults have witnessed homophobic bullying in schools.

⇨ Almost one in seven people has witnessed homophobic bullying in the workplace.
⇨ 75 per cent of *Sun* readers think that prejudice against gay people in Britain should be tackled.
⇨ Liberal Democrat voters are most likely to think that politicians are likely to conceal their sexual orientation.

Ben Summerskill, Stonewall Chief Executive, said: 'We wanted to establish whether the shrill voices in modern Britain still opposing equality are actually representative. While a significant majority of Britons are clearly not prejudiced, as this polling demonstrates, their voices are often drowned out by a minority who are.

---

73 per cent said that anti-gay prejudice needed addressing

'I'm delighted we now have hard evidence that people don't want to live in a society that allows prejudice against any group of people, including lesbians and gay men, to fester.'
14 May 2007

⇨ The above information is reprinted with kind permission from Stonewall. Visit www.stonewall.org. uk for more information.

© Stonewall

Does sexual orientation discrimination apply to me?

Information from the Commission for Equality and Human Rights

Legal protection from discrimination on the basis of sexual orientation applies to everyone, whatever their sexual orientation.

Sexual orientation discrimination includes being treated less favourably because:
⇨ you are lesbian, gay, bisexual or straight;
⇨ people think you are lesbian, gay, bisexual or straight, or
⇨ you are associated with someone who is lesbian, gay, bisexual or straight, for example a friend, relative or colleague.

The law applies to direct and indirect discrimination as well as to harassment and victimisation. The law applies to the private, public and not-for-profit sectors.

⇨ The above information is reprinted with kind permission from the Commission for Equality and Human Rights. Visit www.equalityhumanrights. com for more information.

© Commission for Equality and Human Rights

Discrimination in employment

Information from Liberty

Many employees or service users suffer discriminatory treatment because they are known or believed to be lesbian, gay, or bisexual. There have also been cases of discriminatory treatment of gay men on the grounds that they may be HIV positive.

Many employees or service users suffer discriminatory treatment because they are known or believed to be lesbian, gay, or bisexual

Until recently a lesbian, gay or bisexual worker was not protected from such treatment by existing UK discrimination legislation, and discrimination on grounds of sexual orientation did not constitute an act of sex discrimination contrary to Sex Discrimination Act 1975 ('SDA').

The position in relation to employment, further and higher education, and vocational training was transformed with the introduction

LIBERTY

PROTECTING CIVIL LIBERTIES
PROMOTING HUMAN RIGHTS

of the Employment Equality (Sexual Orientation) Regulations 2003 ('Sexual Orientation Regulations 2003'). These gave effect to a European Union Directive extending the equality provisions to sexual minorities not previously protected by Community law, and came into force on 1 December 2003.

The Sexual Orientation Regulations 2007 include protection against discrimination on the grounds of being in a civil partnership. In the fields of employment and training, similar protection is provided under the SDA.

What is sexual orientation discrimination?

The Sexual Orientation Regulations 2003 and the Equalities Act 2006 (which introduced the Sexual Orientation Regulations 2007) define sexual orientation as a 'sexual orientation toward persons of the same sex, persons of the opposite sex, or persons of the same sex and the opposite sex'. Accordingly the regulations prohibit discrimination against not just lesbians and gay men, but heterosexual and bisexual people as well. Both regulations include perceived sexual orientation, to address a situation where someone is discriminated against because he or she is thought to be gay or lesbian. This definition enables gay applicants not to have to 'come out' in order to bring a claim, and also protects those heterosexual applicants that become the subject of stereotypical homophobic assumptions about appearance or manner.

There are four types of discrimination: direct discrimination, indirect discrimination, victimisation and harassment. There is no need for such discrimination to be intentional or overt. Tribunals and courts have long-recognised the hidden nature of much discrimination.

Both regulations apply to aiding unlawful acts by another and vicarious liability by either an employer or the service provider.

Direct discrimination

Direct discrimination occurs when, on the ground of your sexual orientation, a person treats you less favourably than he or she treats or would treat other persons. The obvious example in employment is where a person is dismissed because of his or her sexuality. In a non-employment situation, this would include refusing to allow a lesbian or gay man to stay in holiday accommodation.

Protection is not limited to circumstances where the less favourable treatment is due to the sexual orientation of the victim, but includes the sexual orientation of others. For example, where an employee is told to discriminate against customers on the

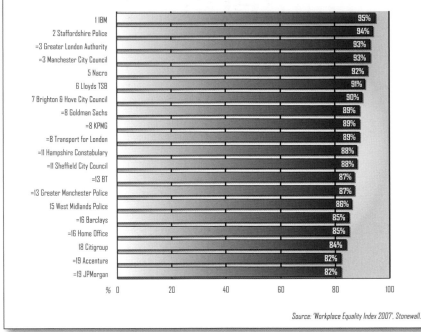

Britain's top 20 LGB employers

Britain's top 20 employers for lesbian and gay staff. 'The Workplace Equality Index (WEI) 2007' features the Top 100 employers in Britain for lesbian and gay people. These are the organisations that scored highest on a 20-question survey covering nine policy and practice areas.

Rank	Employer	%
1	IBM	95%
2	Staffordshire Police	94%
=3	Greater London Authority	93%
=3	Manchester City Council	93%
5	Nacro	92%
6	Lloyds TSB	91%
7	Brighton & Hove City Council	90%
=8	Goldman Sachs	89%
=8	KPMG	89%
=8	Transport for London	89%
=11	Hampshire Constabulary	88%
=11	Sheffield City Council	88%
=13	BT	87%
=13	Greater Manchester Police	87%
15	West Midlands Police	86%
=16	Barclays	85%
=16	Home Office	85%
18	Citigroup	84%
=19	Accenture	82%
=19	JPMorgan	82%

Source: 'Workplace Equality Index 2007', Stonewall.

grounds of their sexual orientation but refuses and is dismissed as a result, the employee can claim under the regulations.

Since the enactment of the Sexual Orientation Regulations 2003, there have been a number of employment tribunal decisions in relation to discrimination and harassment of lesbian and gay men. Most involved overt homophobic language, and homophobic treatment over a period of time. However, there is no requirement for discrimination to be overt or even conscious.

Indirect discrimination

Indirect discrimination occurs when an employer or service provider imposes a specific provision, criterion or practice which, though it may apply equally to persons of any sexual orientation, does in fact place people of the same sexual orientation as you at a particular disadvantage. To rely on the regulations you must have personally suffered that disadvantage. The employer or service provider may be able to argue that the disadvantage was justified, but only if it is a proportionate means of achieving a legitimate end.

The most obvious example of potential indirect discrimination would be the provision of benefits by reference to marital status, since same-sex couples cannot marry. It is now no longer lawful to provide such benefits to married persons without providing equal access to such benefits for civil partners, unless the right accrued prior to the introduction of the Civil Partnership Act, or the benefit relates to period of service prior to the introduction of the Civil Partnership Act.

There are four types of discrimination: direct discrimination, indirect discrimination, victimisation and harassment

---

Victimisation

Victimisation occurs when one person treats you less favourably than he or she treats, or would treat, someone else in those particular circumstances because you have done any of the following:

⇨ brought proceedings against the discriminator or any other person under the regulations;
⇨ given evidence or information in connection with proceedings brought by any person against the discriminator or any other person under the regulations;
⇨ otherwise done anything under or by reference to the regulations in relation to the discriminator or any other person; or
⇨ alleged that the discriminator or any other person has committed an act which (whether or not the allegation so states) would amount to a contravention of the regulations.

Victimisation also occurs where you are treated less favourably because the discriminator knows or suspects that you intend to do any of those things.

Allegations of discrimination must be made in good faith in order to be protected by the victimisation provisions of the regulations.

Harassment

Harassment on the grounds of sexual orientation is a separate unlawful act. The Sexual Orientation Regulations 2003 (but not under the Sexual Orientation Regulations 2007) make it unlawful for a person to subject you to harassment on the grounds of your sexual orientation. Harassment is defined as unwanted conduct which has the purpose or effect of violating your dignity, or creating an intimidating, hostile, degrading, humiliating or offensive workplace environment for you.

In considering claims of harassment, the Employment Tribunal must consider whether the conduct would reasonably be considered as having that effect in all the circumstances, as well as the particular perception of the person bringing the claim. The requirement of reasonableness introduces an objective element to the consideration of harassment, rather than just relying on whether the victim genuinely felt harassed. As harassment is a separate unlawful act, it is not necessary to point to a comparator.

A victim of harassment may also have a separate claim under the Protection of Harassment Act 1997.

⇨ The above information is re-printed with kind permission from Liberty. Visit www.yourrights.org.uk for more information.

© Liberty

'Pink plateau' blocks path to top for gay executives

By Patrick Collinson

It's called the 'pink plateau'. It's the glass ceiling that makes gay men and lesbians virtually invisible in the boardrooms of global multinationals.

Homophobia may be withering in offices and on the shopfloor but among Britain's business elite the closet remains firmly shut. At the global oil majors, routinely negotiating deals in countries not known for their tolerance of homosexuality, being openly gay is simply not an option.

> It's called the 'pink plateau'. It's the glass ceiling that makes gay men and lesbians virtually invisible in the boardrooms of global multinationals

'There still isn't a single openly gay person running a FTSE 100 company in Britain,' said Ben Summerskill, chief executive of lobbying group Stonewall.

A recent survey of the country's top 100 most influential gay and lesbian people named only three chief executives willing to have their names published, led by Sir Michael Bishop, head of the airline BMI.

Mission statements embracing equality appear to apply to employees, not directors. Even among the top gay-friendly employers celebrated in Stonewall's annual Workplace Equality Index, only seven had an openly gay member on their board of directors or in senior management.

'If you look at figures such as Sir Michael Bishop or [Labour Lord] Waheed Alli, the one thing that makes them stand out is that they did it by themselves. Successful business people who are gay or from ethnic minorities are disproportionately self-made entrepreneurs. That's because they don't see career progression within a conventional corporate structure,' said Mr Summerskill.

Neither BP nor Shell appear in Stonewall's index, nor any of the global mining companies that make up a large part of the FTSE 100.

BP has its headquarters in London and its gay workers are protected by UK anti-discrimination legislation. Recently, it even formalised an internal network for gay staff. But its global operations put openly homosexual staff climbing the corporate ladder in an invidious position. The career path inside a multinational oil company follows a route through the world's petroleum production centres, taking in the Middle East, Russia and sub-Saharan Africa, locations where homosexuality is at best socially unacceptable and at worst punishable by death. BP's roots are in Iran, which has executed thousands of gay men since the Islamic revolution.

Oil industry executives say that while Lord Browne's homosexuality was 'an open secret', his decision to keep it out of the public glare was understandable. His job was to hammer out multibillion-pound deals with the likes of Colonel Gadafy of Libya and President Putin of Russia. Libya punishes homosexuality with five years in jail; in Russia it was recently decriminalised and removed from the list of mental disorders.

One senior male gay oil executive, who did not wish to be named, said yesterday: 'It's still a very macho environment. Oil companies will "manage" your career, sending you to various locations around the world and if it's a choice between a white heterosexual male and someone else, you'll lose out. There are always issues about the culture in overseas locations and whether you'll be accepted.

'This is also an industry where a lot of business takes place outside the office workplace; in people's home, hotels and so on. If you're gay, you're not going to be invited into the inner sanctum. In my last company I was, pointedly, never invited to the Christmas dinner for senior executives and their wives.'

But he said there were signs of improvement. 'I know of postings recently where a man and his male partner have been sent out to countries in Asia by the company. There's more of a pragmatic approach.'

2 May 2007

© Guardian Newspapers Limited 2007

⇨ According to current scientific and professional understanding, the core attractions that form the basis for adult sexual orientation typically emerge between middle childhood and early adolescence. These patterns of emotional, romantic, and sexual attraction may arise without any prior sexual experience. (page 1)

⇨ Both heterosexual behaviour and homosexual behaviour are normal aspects of human sexuality. Both have been documented in many different cultures and historical eras. (page 3)

⇨ 16% of men and 15% of women surveyed by Ipsos MORI reported having sexual contact with someone of the same sex as themselves. (page 4)

⇨ Only one in 100 Britons would describe themselves as gay, according to the first government research into the nation's sexuality. (page 5)

⇨ Several studies have found there to be a genetic influence on the determining of one's sexuality – whether it be the levels of one's hormones or the size of certain parts of the brain (i.e. the corpus callosum or medulla oblongata). However, there is no conclusive proof that homosexuality is completely determined by genetic factors. (page 6)

⇨ Some people think that people who describe themselves as bisexual are really gay but cannot admit this. This is not true; you can be attracted to both boys and girls and being bisexual is not the same as being gay. It is also not true that bisexual people are really straight but just experimenting. (page 10)

⇨ Seven out of ten young lesbian and gay people say homophobic bullying affects their schoolwork. (page 15)

⇨ Homophobic bullying is almost endemic in Britain's schools. Almost two-thirds (65 per cent) of young lesbian, gay and bisexual pupils have experienced direct bullying. Seventy-five per cent of young gay people attending faith schools have experienced homophobic bullying. (page 17)

⇨ Seventy per cent of teachers and lecturers report hearing terms such as gay, bitch, slag, poof, batty boy, queer and lezzie used in sexist or homophobic bullying in their school or college, according to an Association of Teachers and Lecturers (ATL) survey. (page 18)

⇨ The gay campaigning organisation Stonewall recently monitored prime-time programming on BBC1 and BBC2 over two weeks and found that, during 168 hours of programming, there were just six minutes that portrayed lesbian and gay lives in a positive manner, as opposed to 32 minutes involving negative terms or contexts. More than half of all the gay references were jokes about sexually predatory or camp and effeminate gay men. (page 24)

⇨ There are a small number of differences between civil partnership and marriage, for example, a civil partnership is registered when the second civil partner signs the relevant document, a civil marriage is registered when the couple exchange spoken words. Opposite-sex couples can opt for a religious or civil marriage ceremony as they choose, whereas formation of a civil partnership will be an exclusively civil procedure. (page 26)

⇨ Localised evidence suggests people are struggling with the ambiguity of language surrounding civil partnerships, and don't know how to refer to their circumstance in social situations, due to a lack of conversational terms that are equivalent to the terms of the traditional marriage. (page 29)

⇨ 43% of people surveyed by YouGov felt that Catholic adoption agencies should not be exempted from the requirement to consider gay couples as potential parents on the same basis as other couples. 29% felt that the Catholic adoption agencies should be exempted, and allowed to reject gay couples wishing to adopt children. Catholic adoption agencies eventually lost their battle to be exempted from the rule to provide equal consideration for gay parents wishing to adopt on 30 January 2007. (page 33)

⇨ The Government has brought forward legislation to tackle discrimination in the provision of goods, facilities and services on grounds of sexual orientation, which came into force on 30 April 2007. (page 35)

⇨ Major new polling commissioned by Stonewall has found that the vast majority of Britons, 85%, support the 2007 Sexual Orientation Regulations, newly-introduced legal protections for gay people. Similar numbers would be happy if a relative, their boss or a footballer in the team they support (92%) was gay, the Living Together survey established. (page 36)

⇨ The Sexual Orientation Regulations 2003 and the Equalities Act 2006 (which introduced the Sexual Orientation Regulations 2007) define sexual orientation as a 'sexual orientation toward persons of the same sex, persons of the opposite sex, or persons of the same sex and the opposite sex'. Accordingly the regulations prohibit discrimination against not just lesbians and gay men, but heterosexual and bisexual people as well. (page 37)

⇨ Stonewall named IBM as the top employer for lesbian and gay staff in 2007. (page 38)

Bisexual

Someone who defines themselves as bisexual or 'bi' is attracted to people of either sex. While a bisexual person may be equally attracted to men and women, this does not have to be the case: they may feel a stronger attraction to one sex than the other, or feel attraction to different sexes at different points in their lives.

Civil partnership

The Civil Partnership Act 2004 (CPA) allowed LGB people the right to form legal partnerships for the first time, giving them rights comparable to those of married couples. A civil partnership is a new legal relationship, exclusively for same-sex couples, distinct from marriage.

Coming out

'Coming out' or 'coming out of the closet' happens when an LGB person feels ready to tell their friends and family about their sexual orientation. As heterosexuality is the most common sexual orientation, those close to them will probably have assumed they were straight. Coming out is a big step for most gay people, especially if they fear a negative reaction from some people. It is quite common for gay people to not be fully 'out', and only let certain people know about their sexuality.

Homophobia

Homophobia is the fear or hatred of homosexuality. Individuals who are homophobic fear or hate the fact that others are sexually attracted to members of their own sex. This fear can lead to behaviour that discriminates against LGBT people and consequently advantages heterosexuals. Such discrimination is illegal under the Equality Act (Sexual Orientation) Regulations 2007.

Heterosexual

Someone who defines themselves as heterosexual is attracted exclusively to people of the opposite sex to themselves. Heterosexuality is the most common sexual orientation. It is often referred to as 'straight'.

Homosexual

Someone who defines themselves as homosexual is attracted exclusively to people of the same sex as themselves. People of this sexual orientation may prefer to call themselves gay, or a lesbian if they are female. While some gay people may use other words such as 'queer' or 'dyke' to describe themselves, these are not considered universally acceptable and other gay people may find them offensive.

Kinsey Scale

The Kinsey Scale, first published in 1948, hypothesises that sexual orientation is not as straightforward as being either gay, straight or bisexual. In other words, it seeks to demonstrate that sexuality is not necessarily clear-cut and can be defined in terms of a scale, on which 0 is exclusively heterosexual, 3 is equally heterosexual and homosexual and 6 is exclusively homosexual, with the other numbers from 0-6 describing states in between.

LGBT

LGBT stands for Lesbian, Gay, Bisexual and Transgender, and is often used as a shorthand way of referring to sexual orientations other than heterosexual. Just LGB (Lesbian, Gay and Bisexual) may also be used.

Pink

The colour pink is often ascribed to issues concerning LGB people. A reference to the 'pink pound', for example, will concern marketing to gay people and how they are likely to spend their money. The 'pink vote' concerns which political parties LGB people are likely to support in elections. The 'pink plateau' is a term coined to describe a problem faced by gay people in the workplace: like the 'glass ceiling' for women, it refers to an inability for a gay person to progress within their chosen field because of discrimination.

Sexuality

The word 'sexuality' is often used interchangeably with 'sexual orientation' in debates concerning LGBT issues. However, it actually has a wider meaning, referring to human sexual behaviour in general.

Sexual orientation

Sexual orientation refers to an enduring pattern of emotional, romantic and/or sexual attractions to men, women or both sexes. Sexual orientation also refers to a person's sense of identity based on those attractions, related behaviours and membership in a community of others who share those attractions. Sexual orientation is usually defined either as heterosexual or 'straight' (attraction to the opposite sex); homosexual or 'gay'/'lesbian' (attraction to the same sex); or bisexual (attraction to both sexes).

Transgender

A transgender person is someone who identifies as the opposite gender than that into which they were born, and who has chosen to live their life in that gender. They may or may not have gone through gender reassignment surgery. Someone's gender identity is separate from their sexual orientation: however, issues concerning transgender people and their rights tend to be discussed in relation to debates about sexuality, as they often suffer similar kinds of discrimination to LGB people. These issues do also cross over into debates concerning equal gender rights, however.

INDEX

Additional Resources

Other Issues titles

If you are interested in researching further some of the issues raised in *Sexual Orientation and Society*, you may like to read the following titles in the **Issues** series:

⇨ Vol. 155 *Domestic Abuse* (ISBN 978 1 86168 442 4)

⇨ Vol. 154 *The Gender Gap* (ISBN 978 1 86168 441 7)

⇨ Vol. 148 *Religious Beliefs* (ISBN 978 1 86168 421 9)

⇨ Vol. 142 *Media Issues* (ISBN 978 1 86168 408 0)

⇨ Vol. 141 *Mental Health* (ISBN 978 1 86168 407 3)

⇨ Vol. 136 *Self-Harm* (ISBN 978 1 86168 388 5)

⇨ Vol. 124 *Parenting Issues* (ISBN 978 1 86168 363 2)

⇨ Vol. 123 *Young People and Health* (ISBN 978 1 86168 362 5)

⇨ Vol. 122 *Bullying* (ISBN 978 1 86168 361 8)

⇨ Vol. 120 *The Human Rights Issue* (ISBN 978 1 86168 353 3)

⇨ Vol. 107 *Work Issues* (ISBN 978 1 86168 327 4)

⇨ Vol. 106 *Trends in Marriage* (ISBN 978 1 86168 326 7)

⇨ Vol. 96 *Preventing Sexual Diseases* (ISBN 978 1 86168 304 5)

For more information about these titles, visit our website at www.independence.co.uk/publicationslist

Useful organisations

You may find the websites of the following organisations useful for further research:

⇨ **About Equal Opportunities:** www.aboutequalopportunities.co.uk

⇨ **American Psychological Association:** www.apa.org

⇨ **ATL:** www.askatl.org.uk

⇨ **Citizens Advice:** www.citizensadvice.org.uk

⇨ **Commission for Equality and Human Rights:** www.equalityhumanrights.com

⇨ **Department for Trade and Industry, Women and Equality Unit:** www.womenandequalityunit.gov.uk

⇨ **Gay Youth Corner:** www.thegyc.com

⇨ **ILGA-Europe:** www.ilga-europe.org

⇨ **Liberty:** www.yourrights.org.uk

⇨ **New Statesman:** www.newstatesman.com

⇨ **Stonewall:** www.stonewall.org.uk

⇨ **Teachernet:** www.teachernet.gov.uk

⇨ **Terrence Higgins Trust:** www.tht.org.uk

⇨ **TheSite:** www.thesite.org

⇨ **YouGov:** www.yougov.com

ACKNOWLEDGEMENTS

The publisher is grateful for permission to reproduce the following material.

While every care has been taken to trace and acknowledge copyright, the publisher tenders its apology for any accidental infringement or where copyright has proved untraceable. The publisher would be pleased to come to a suitable arrangement in any such case with the rightful owner.

Chapter One: Sexuality Issues

Answers to your questions, © American Psychological Association, Exploring your sexuality, © TheSite, Just one in 100 tells researchers: I'm gay, © Telegraph Group Ltd, Theories, © Stonewall, I am what I am and it's not a choice, © New Statesman Ltd, When coming out goes wrong, © TheSite.org, Parents of gay children, © Nigel Cooper, Bisexual, © Terrence Higgins Trust, Girls who like boys... and girls, © Melanie Ashby, The wrong label?, © TheSite, Transgender, © Terrence Higgins Trust, Homophobia in the classroom, © About Equal Opportunities, Homophobic bullying, © Crown copyright is reproduced with the permission of Her Majesty's Stationery Office, Sad to be gay, © Guardian Newspapers Ltd, The school report, © Stonewall, Prevalence of homophobia in schools, © ATL, The prince married a man, and lived happily ever after, © Guardian Newspapers Ltd, Making babies the gay way, © Nigel Cooper, Gay adoption, © First Post, Homosexuality in the media: is the press good?, © Gay Youth Corner, Disappearing act, © New Statesman Ltd.

Chapter Two: Sexuality and the Law

Civil Partnership Act 2004, © Crown copyright is reproduced with the permission of Her Majesty's Stationery Office, Are civil partnerships really civil?, © Citizens Advice, Civil partnerships fall by 55%, © Local Government Association, The European Convention and Court of Human Rights, © Stonewall, Gay adoption in Europe, © ILGA-Europe, Church loses opt-out fight over gay adoptions, © Telegraph Group Ltd, The right to equal treatment: parental rights, © Liberty, Sexual orientation legislation, © Crown copyright is reproduced with the permission of Her Majesty's Stationery Office, Support for LGBT legal protection, © Stonewall, Does sexual orientation discrimination apply to me?, © Commission for Equality and Human Rights, Discrimination in Employment, © Liberty, 'Pink plateau' blocks path to top for gay executives, © Guardian Newspapers Ltd.

Photographs

Flickr: pages 22a (Ed Hill), 23 (switch_1010), 35 (Kevin Halstead).
Stock Xchng: pages 8 (Marcia Almeida), 9 (Dez Pain), 12a (Scott Snyder), 12b (Koos Schwaneberg), 14 (Tory Byrne), 22b (Bianca de Blok).
Wikimedia Commons: pages 19 (Jon Ward), 26 (David Ludwig).

Illustrations

Pages 1, 20, 37: Angelo Madrid; pages 3, 25: Bev Aisbett; pages 6, 13, 34: Simon Kneebone; pages 11, 21, 39: Don Hatcher.

Additional editorial by Claire Owen, on behalf of Independence Educational Publishers.

And with thanks to the team: Mary Chapman, Sandra Dennis, Claire Owen and Jan Sunderland.

Lisa Firth
Cambridge
April, 2008